What Leaders Are Saying

"James Goll understands that God's heart for and covenant with Israel and the Jewish people is the vital link that binds together His global purposes. In this dynamic book he calls us to pray from an eternal perspective for the temporal situations that face Israel on a daily basis. Israel is the centerpiece of God's timeline and the center of attention in global affairs. James calls us to take our place as watchmen over the 'apple of God's eye.'"

Robert Stearns, founder and executive director, Eagles' Wings;
founder, Day of Prayer for the Peace of Jerusalem

"Intercession results when one understands the times and knows what to do about them. That is what this book accomplishes. This is fresh. This is today. This is crucial. This is happening on our watch. This will appeal to a ready heart."

Bill McCartney, founder/chairman, The Road to Jerusalem

"As an evangelist I have found that going to the Jew first opens up a greater supernatural door for Gentile revival. We are at the fullness of the Gentile age, which means God is removing the spiritual scales from the eyes of Jewish people. James Goll's instruction on praying for Israel will trigger the great Jewish and Arab revival. This will result in the greatest Gentile revival in history!"

Sid Roth, president, Messianic Vision

"James W. Goll's book weaves scriptural truth with prophetic insights into a powerful book of instruction on praying for Israel in a way that impacts Arabs and all the nations. I wholeheartedly recommend not only the reading but the implementation of his guidelines for prayer. It's a well-presented prayer aid for all who embrace God's call on the covenant nation as well as for those who are at work among the nations, yet know that it all started and finishes in Jerusalem."

Don Finto, pastor emeritus, Belmont Church, Nashville;
author, *My People Shall Be Your People*

"*Praying for Israel's Destiny* presents a timely sweep of what God is saying regarding Israel in this day and hour. For all those who love and pray for the apple of the Lord's eye, this is a must-read."

Cindy Jacobs, co-founder, Generals International

"With a history of more than 25 years of interceding as a watchman for Israel, James Goll has a heart that burns to see the fulfillment of God's purposes for His people and His land come to pass. In his newest book, *Praying for Israel's Destiny*, James not only shares the prophetic insights and understanding of God's destiny for Israel that he has received over the years, but he provides intercessors with a roadmap for praying the Scriptures in agreement with God's heart for those He calls 'the apple of His eye.' A timely and significant book!"

Jane Hansen, president/CEO, Aglow International

"This fine guide for prayer for Israel deserves wide use. I hope and trust that it will indeed be a manual of prayer for Israel for many believers. The joining of biblical patterns of prayer and their application for the contemporary situation is especially helpful."

Daniel Juster, director, Tikkun International, Jerusalem

"This book is a refreshing combination of a spirit of revelation, biblical clarity, a heart for Israel and Scripture-based prayers that will serve the global prayer movement well for such a time as this. *Praying for Israel's Destiny* should be used as a text in prayer meetings and prayer rooms across the nations."

Mike Bickle, director, International House of Prayer of Kansas City

"In Romans 10:1 the apostle Paul shared that his 'heart's desire and *prayer* for Israel is that they might be saved.' Now, more than at any time in history, Christians need to be praying for God's plans and purposes for Israel and the Jewish people to be fulfilled. I consider *Praying for Israel's Destiny* to be an important tool to accomplish this."

Jonathan Bernis, president and executive director,
Jewish Voice Ministries International

PRAYING FOR ISRAEL'S DESTINY

Effective Intercession for God's Purposes in the Middle East

JAMES W. GOLL

Chosen
Grand Rapids, Michigan

Published by Chosen Books
a division of Baker Publishing Group
P.O. Box 6287, Grand Rapids, MI 49516-6287
www.chosenbooks.com

Second printing, May 2005

Printed in the United States of America

Library of Congress Cataloging-in-Publication Data

Goll, Jim W.
Praying for Israel's destiny : effective intercession for God's purposes in the Middle East / James W. Goll.
p. cm.
Includes bibliographical references and index.
ISBN 0-8007-9369-2 (pbk. : alk. paper)
1. Israel (Christian theology) 2. Judaism (Christian theology) 3. Intercessory prayer—Christianity. I. Title.
BT93.G656 2005
231.7′6—dc22 2004024518

Contents

Foreword by Bill McCartney 7
Dedication and Acknowledgments 9

Part 1 Praying for Spiritual Understanding
1. Appointed a Watchman for Israel 13
2. Character to Carry the Burden 29
3. A Heart Like These 45

Part 2 Praying for the Descendants of Abraham
4. The Descendants of Hagar 63
5. The Descendants of Sarah 77
6. The Descendants of Keturah 91

Part 3 Praying for the Fullness of God's Purposes
7. Jerusalem: A City of Destiny 107
8. Praying for the Fulfillment of *Aliyah* 123
9. God's Road Map for Israel's Future 139

Appendix: The Cry Yearly Prayer Focus 155
Notes 157
Glossary 161
Referral Ministries 165
Recommended Reading 169
For More Information 171
Index 173

Foreword

Isn't a book supposed to get better with each chapter? I mean, aren't you supposed to be drawn in and fully intrigued?

If this is your expectation, then get cozy, light up the fireplace and let the Holy Spirit minister deeply to your soul. James W. Goll surely wrote this under the influence! I have been educated, challenged, nourished and provoked.

Intercession results when one understands the times and knows what to do about them. That is what this book accomplishes. This is fresh. This is today. This is crucial. This is happening on our watch. This will appeal to a ready heart.

Henry Blackaby was quoted as saying, "Find out what God is doing and join Him." This is our chance!

Bill McCartney, founder/chairman
The Road to Jerusalem

Dedication and Acknowledgments

With a heart of deep gratitude, I give thanks for the team efforts that have prevailed to birth *Praying for Israel's Destiny* for such a time as this. Thanks go to our weekly Israel Prayer Watch and our Network Prayer Warriors who prayed me through on this one. Blessings go to David Sluka, who became my right-hand man for this task. Deep appreciation goes to the staff of Encounters Network (formerly Ministry to the Nations) and my dear family for standing with me.

Blessings to Jane Campbell and the team at Chosen Books for not giving up on me when our family went through many personal trials as this book unfolded. I am indebted to my teachers and mentors over the years. Your shadows have touched my life. Thank you!

It is with a heart filled with honor that I dedicate this book to all believers in the land of Israel who live this message out every day. I honor your pioneering intercession, your perseverance and your labors of love for our Messiah and the Jewish people. May He truly strengthen and bless you as you labor in His vineyard!

May the Spirit of revelation rest on each one who reads this book and may many new recruits be raised up as Watchmen on the Walls for the Lord and Jerusalem's sake.

With a heart to pray,
James W. Goll
Encounters Network
Franklin, TN

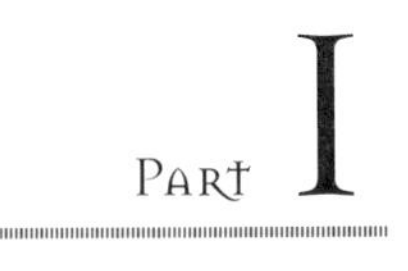

Part I

Praying for Spiritual Understanding

I
Appointed a Watchman for Israel

> On your walls, O Jerusalem, I have appointed watchmen;
> All day and all night they will never keep silent.
> You who remind the LORD, take no rest for yourselves;
> And give Him no rest until He establishes
> And makes Jerusalem a praise in the earth.
>
> Isaiah 62:6–7

Have you ever missed a strategic appointment? Or have you ever realized at the last minute that you were about to miss an important engagement unless you kicked into action right away? I have, and it is an experience I do not care to relive! It is like waking up out of a stupor; all of a sudden you remember your appointment, and then you rush around like a chicken with your head cut off! If you miss the appointment altogether, you are filled with emotions and thoughts of disappointment, anger, sorrow and even "Why did I do that!" But if you are awake, prepared and ready for the appointments on your calendar, then a sense of destiny fulfilled, satisfaction and anticipation for what comes next arises within you.

Did you know that God has a calendar with appointments waiting to be fulfilled? Watchmen remind God of the appointments on His calendar that have not been fully met and fulfilled. The task of a watchman is by "appointment." It means being chosen for the divine privilege of composing history before the throne of the Almighty.

I want to be a history maker! That is the goal of my life. Are you ready to make a difference? The recipe for enduring change is that simple. Yes, prayer changes things![1] Are you taking your biblical place on the walls for Israel's sake? The call for watchmen went out in Isaiah's time, and the Holy Spirit is releasing this strategic call again in the 21st century.

It seems as if God has been conducting a monumental chess game throughout the ages, waiting for the strategic moment in history to make His move. Yes, the playing board has been set, and the pieces have been chosen. This call for watchmen is the strategic positioning of His intercessory knights and prophetic bishops being brought together for a sweeping move—one that all the world will observe closely. No eye will miss the mysterious and fascinating time. Therefore we must pray for our eyes to be opened with His spiritual understanding.

Seeing through God's Eyes

The first conference that my wife, Michal Ann, and I hosted in Nashville, Tennessee, was on the "Mystery of the Church of Israel." Our friends Avner and Rachel Boskey of Final Frontier Ministries located in Beersheva, Israel, led the worship. During one of the worship times, I saw an open vision of an eye staring right at me. In the middle of this eye, I saw the Star of David. As I gazed more intently upon the vision, I saw a Scripture reference written in the middle of the Star of David. The Scripture that I saw was Zechariah 2:8.

At that time I did not have the foggiest idea what "Zechariah 2:8" referred to. So I turned in my Bible to Zechariah and read the following: "For he who touches you [Israel], touches the apple of His eye." Some other translations render the phrase "apple of God's eye" as "the *pupil* of God's eye." So the *apple* of the eye is the *pupil*, and the pupil of the eye is the instrument through which one sees. He who touches Israel touches the center of God's eye—the center of God's sight.

If you want to have an accurate prophetic perception of life, Scripture and God's purposes in the Earth—especially in the days before Christ returns—you must have God's vision. You must see through God's eyes and then hold dear to your heart the things that are closest to the heart of God. Since Israel is at the center of God's vision, we will need to see through the lens of Israel's destiny if we are to see correctly and clearly. Please understand that this is not an ethnic issue. This is a God issue. The primary issue is not about a race of people. This is about a promise-keeping God who is faithful to fulfill His plan for a people, a city and a nation through which He has chosen to display His splendor. This is about God's faithful character being on lavish display for all to observe and know.

A phrase in a famous hymn says, "His eye is on the sparrow and I know He watches me." Well, if God's eye is on the sparrows, then you know His gaze has never lifted from the center of His attention. That center is Israel, and His eye is ever gazing on them.

It is time for the unveiling of the mystery of Israel as the apple of God's eye, the centerpiece of attention on God's chessboard.[2] I have been interceding as a watchman for Israel for well over 25 years. From this vantage point I would like to share with you seven reasons why I pray and take a stand for Israel. I believe that you, too, should be a watchman on the walls who cries out to God on Israel's behalf. Ready for your assignment?

Seven Reasons Why I Pray and Take a Stand for Israel

1. Israel Is Still the Apple of God's Eye and His Inheritance

Pray and take a stand for Israel because Israel is still very close to God's heart. I have already shared Zechariah 2:8, which says, "He who touches you [Israel], touches the apple of His eye." Centuries before Zechariah prophesied these words, Moses wrote a song containing a very similar picture:

> For the LORD's portion is His people;
> Jacob [Israel] is the allotment of His inheritance. . . .
> He encircled him, He cared for him,
> He guarded him as the pupil of His eye. . . .
> He spread His wings and caught them,
> He carried them on His pinions.
>
> Deuteronomy 32:9–11

Psalm 148:14 declares, "And He has lifted up a horn for His people, praise for all His godly ones; even for the sons of Israel, a people near to Him." Did you hear that? "A people near to Him." I love that!

The first reason I pray for Israel is not profound. I pray for Israel because I want to be close to God's heart and I want to be in alignment with God's sight. If God says that Israel is the apple or pupil of His eye, then I want to pray with insight—with His sight. Do you want to be close to the heart of God? Then be close to the things, people and purposes that are close to His heart. Fulfill your appointment. Take a stand and be a watchman for Israel!

2. It Is Time to Have Compassion

Pray for Israel by being filled with compassion for Israel's condition. Psalm 102:13–14 says:

> You will arise and have compassion on Zion;
> For it is time to be gracious to her,
> For the appointed time has come.
> Surely Your servants find pleasure in her stones
> And feel pity for her dust.

The time has come!

When I recorded the vocal prayer tracks for *Prayers for Israel*, I was in a small, out-of-the-way studio in Kelowna, British Columbia, Canada. It was, frankly, chilly in that little building! But while I was praying through Psalm 102 for the cut "It's Time to Have Compassion," the Holy Spirit came upon me and my heart burned with the fire of God. I started to weep. Perhaps I was releasing a measure of God's heart at that moment. You see, God wants us to pray, not with a clenched fist of self-righteous anger, but with a compassionate heart. I have cried out to the Lord to tenderize my heart. You, too, can ask the Holy Spirit to give you His heart of compassion for Israel.

I was asked in a recent interview what my prayer times are like. I thought, *How can I answer that? Prayer has taken so many different forms over the years.* I said something like this:

> Well, I started out by praying the Word, and engrafted the Word into my life. I prayed the Scriptures for hours. Then I came to a time where I learned to worship and sing and pray in the Spirit. I was taught by my tutor, the Holy Spirit, to pick up the warrior's mantle of prophetic intercession and exercise the authority of a believer in Christ. This led to another turn in the journey of prayer—prayer of the heart that does not even have language form. It is simply being there with Him. But the primary way that I pray today is with tears. Something happens inside and I just begin to weep. God puts

> in me His contrite heart, and I begin to feel what God feels over a situation, a place, an individual or a group of people.

God wants to give His heart to us so that we can pray over Israel with compassion. The time has come for us to receive His heart so that our prayers will go far beyond merely saying correct words and on into the prayer of the heart—even to the prayer of tears. It is time to have compassion on Zion. That is why I pray and take a stand for Israel. Want to join me?

3. God Commands Us to Give Him and Ourselves No Rest

Pray and take a stand for Israel because God wants to establish Jerusalem and make her a praise in the Earth. The prophet Isaiah declared:

> On your walls, O Jerusalem, I have appointed watchmen;
> All day and all night they will never keep silent.
> You who remind the Lord, take no rest for yourselves;
> And give Him no rest until He establishes
> And makes Jerusalem a praise in the earth.
>
> Isaiah 62:6–7

Give Him no rest until *what* is established? *Jerusalem!* He did not say Washington DC, Paris or London. He did not say Constantinople, Athens, Damascus, Moscow or Cairo. He said until *Jerusalem* is made a praise. A what? A *praise*! Many news reports will tell you that Jerusalem is far from being a praise in the Earth. Many people curse Jerusalem and call the Jewish people names I will not even dare repeat. So we must lift our voices in prayer until she becomes a praise—a glorious praise—in all the Earth.

Now we must understand something very clearly: This is not for our sake! It is for Zion's sake! It is not about what is convenient. It is a priority! Our ministry hosts weekly prayer watches for Israel. It is not always easy, but it is a delight!

No form of prayer is convenient, but as you put your hand to this plow you will find that even more distractions come your way. Reasons not to pray will appear, reasons to take your ease, distractions, interruptions in your schedule. Just set your heart to be resolute. Pray until!

4. God Desires to Work through Us for Israel's Salvation

Pray for Israel so that Israel will be saved. I have shared that God wants to give us His heart of compassion—His tears—for Israel. But tears and compassion are not God's end objective. God wants us to receive His heart so that we can pray with accuracy and discernment for the salvation of Israel. The apostle Paul said, "I have great sorrow and unceasing grief in my heart. . . . My heart's desire and my prayer to God for them is for their salvation" (Romans 9:2; 10:1). Paul also declared, "I could wish that I myself were accursed . . . for the sake of my brethren . . . who are Israelites" (Romans 9:3–4). Paul was willing to be separated from Christ so that his brethren might know their Messiah. What a sacrifice Paul was willing to make for the sake of Israel!

At the conferences that our ministry hosts, we normally include a special Israel Prayer Watch so that believers can listen, agree, receive, learn and participate. At one of these Israel Prayer Watches, I was given a wonderful, interactive visionary encounter. I entered into rays of God's brilliant white light. As I stepped into this light, I saw a man standing at the end of a tunnel of God's vast love. Then, suddenly, it was as though my being was soaring in the air and leapt into the heart of the man standing in the light of God's love. An apostolic heart of God was pounding loudly within him. Words in rhythm with the heartbeat of God were echoing in the heart of this man, who appeared to be a representation of Paul the apostle. Then I heard, "My heart's desire is that all Israel be saved." My own heart was pierced once again. I wept and wept for Israel's salvation.

I have read this verse from the book of Romans many times. I have fasted and prayed much over the years for Israel's sake. But this experience cemented into my being what is of utmost importance. We must pray for Israel's salvation to go forth like a torch that is burning. God has desires—the apostle Paul had desires—do you pray with a burning heart of desire for Israel's salvation?

5. God Commands Us to Pray for the Peace of Jerusalem

Pray and take a stand for Israel because God wants to bless Jerusalem and her inhabitants with His peace and goodness. David, the warrior psalmist, loved Jerusalem and fought many battles for her. Wars and heated conflicts still rage today over this piece of land in the Middle East. David's exhortation in Psalm 122 must still be prayed and sung today: "May they prosper who love you. May peace be within your walls, and prosperity within your palaces."

Consider God's heart as revealed in many other psalms:

> You hear, O Lord, the desire of the afflicted;
> you encourage them, and you listen to their cry,
> defending the fatherless and the oppressed,
> in order that man, who is of the earth, may terrify no more.
>
> Psalm 10:17–18, NIV

> Blessed is he who has regard for the weak;
> the Lord delivers him in times of trouble.
>
> Psalm 41:1, NIV

> I know that the Lord secures justice for the poor
> and upholds the cause of the needy.
>
> Psalm 140:12, NIV

The apostle Paul also loved Jerusalem and was concerned for the city and for the welfare of her inhabitants. In his letter to the Romans, Paul wrote the following:

> But now, I am going to Jerusalem serving the saints. For Macedonia and Achaia have been pleased to make a contribution for the poor among the saints in Jerusalem. Yes, they were pleased to do so, and they are indebted to them. For if the Gentiles have shared in their spiritual things, they are indebted to minister to them also in material things.
>
> Romans 15:25–27

Today, with all of the hundreds of thousands of new immigrants, tourism on a downturn, tension and pressures, terrorism, wars and rumors of wars, Israel's economy has been absolutely devastated. We must pray for the *shalom* of God for the city of peace. But we must do more. I have often quoted intercessor S. D. Gordon: "You can do more than pray after you've prayed. But you cannot do more than pray until you have prayed."

It is time for our works to match our faith. The Joseph Storehouse, led by Barry and Batya Segal in Israel, is a wonderful present-day example of ministries coming together to partner and put feet to their faith and compassion. They are walking out God's heart for Jewish and Arab people in a very practical way. I have had the blessing of partnering with the Israel Relief Fund and other entities, seeing millions of dollars of aid—medical equipment, food, clothing and other needed supplies—sent from the evangelical community to those in need in the land of Israel.

May God bless these and other ministries, and raise up many more to feed and clothe the poor and to give a cup of water to "the least of these my brethren"—Jesus' brothers after the flesh.

6. Israel's Acceptance of Jesus Will Bring Life

Pray and act for Israel because the Jewish people's acceptance of the Messiah Jesus will lead to worldwide revival of unprecedented magnitude. Romans 11:15 says, "For if [Israel's] rejection [of Christ] is the reconciliation of the world, what will their acceptance be but life from the dead?" Wow! Life from the dead!

Isaiah prophesied, "In the days to come Jacob will take root, Israel will blossom and sprout and they will fill the whole earth with fruit" (Isaiah 27:6). This is more than just natural fruit! Praying for Israel is one of the major keys to world revival. As the Jewish people are awakened out of their sleep and behold their Messiah, this will create a divine acceleration into a time when hundreds of thousands, if not literally millions, turn to Jesus as their Messiah. There is nothing more potent than a Jewish believer telling others about the God of Abraham, Isaac and Jacob. Want to see worldwide revival? Then pray!

Israel's acceptance of the glorious Messiah will be used to catalyze the greatest spiritual awakening that this planet has ever seen. The whole Earth will be filled with the fruit of revival. I pray toward this end! Will you join me?

7. Jesus Linked His Second Coming to Israel's Turning to Him

Pray and take a stand for Israel because the Second Coming of Christ is linked to Israel's response to Him. Jesus prophesied before His death, "For I say to you, from now on you will not see Me until you say, 'Blessed is He who comes in the name of the Lord!'" (Matthew 23:39). Jesus linked His Second Coming to Israel's national returning, or turning, to Him.

Johannes Facius, chief executive and operational head of Ebenezer Emergency Fund International, has also helped to launch prayer initiatives in 45 nations of the Earth. Johannes declares:

> Now get the picture here! The Lord is not saying to the Jewish inhabitants of the city of Jerusalem that they shall never see Him again. He is saying that they shall not see Him until they are ready to welcome Him. When He came the first time He was not welcomed. The Messiah has no intention of repeating this situation. Jesus is saying that His Second Coming will not take place until there is a Jewish population in Jerusalem who will welcome Him with all of their hearts. Before that can happen, the descendants of the Jews who were exiled nearly two-thousand years ago will have to return to Jerusalem.[3]

Do you want to see Jesus come back in your lifetime? Is it possible to hasten the day of His appearing? (See 2 Peter 3:12.) Do you want to see Jesus come again? Then pray that the blinders on the Jewish people's eyes will fall off (see Romans 11:25) and that they will welcome their Messiah with open hearts.

Anna and Simeon spent their time in the Temple preparing the way for the first coming of our glorious Savior and Lord (see Luke 2:25–38). So will it be before the Second Coming of our glorious Messiah. Hundreds and thousands of Annas and Simeons will arise across the nations, taking their place in temple ministry of worship and intercession, with watching and fasting, preparing the way for the Second Advent of our Jewish Messiah, *Yeshua*.

Why pray and take a stand of action for Israel? Because Jesus said to, because Isaiah said to, because David the psalmist said to and because today the Holy Spirit is saying to. There may be many other reasons to pray and act for Israel. Pick whatever reason you want, but pray and take a stand for Israel!

Launching the Cry for Israel's Sake!

God wants us to know His heart for Israel and to be filled with compassion for Israel's condition. He also desires that this compassion provoke us to cry out to Him about what is on His heart. The good news is that the Lord answers when we cry out to Him for help. Israel's history shows a clear pattern of people who, time and again, found themselves in trouble, cried out to the Lord and saw Him deliver them out of their adversity.

It is my conviction, and also that of many other leaders in the Body of the Messiah, that the Holy Spirit is opening a strategic window of opportunity for the Gentile church to arise "for such a time as this." We must pray and take a stand as never before in all our Church history. We must pray for God's purposes to be fulfilled in Israel, in the Jewish people and in all the descendants of Abraham.

The Church is in this pivotal hour recovering the lost weapon of fasting. Spiritual crisis intervention is launched from the biblical foundation of prayer with fasting. God's Word provides many examples of this, but perhaps the greatest is that of Esther and Mordecai, who, in a time of life-and-death crisis, called a solemn three-day assembly from all food and drink. God provided them with a way of escape, and He will provide one for Israel today if we respond as they did.

The Holy Spirit is calling us to be modern-day Esthers and Mordecais on behalf of God's ancient covenant people. Therefore, with faith, humility and a sense of destiny and urgency, I am calling for three days of prayer with fasting, named *The Cry*, every year during the time of Purim until God's purpose and destiny is completed among His people Israel. It is time to take a stand!

According to the Jewish calendar, Purim is held in the month of *Adar*, which usually falls in February or March. Moses was born in *Adar*. It is also the month when the Jewish leader Maccabees defeated the Syrians and the month when the orders were given to rebuild the walls of Jerusalem preceding the reconstruction of the Temple and the first return of the Jewish people to Israel.[4] (Dates for the feast of Purim, according to the Julian calendar, appear in the appendix along with supporting Scripture. These dates are written out for the next several years and are the days for The Cry to arise annually.)

Will you join me? The Holy Spirit is issuing a prophetic invitation into history-making intercession. When we earnestly seek the heart of God concerning the Jewish people and their destiny, we unlock historic action. Ready to lift The Cry to the Lord with me? Let's pray until Israel's destiny is fully met and fulfilled!

Target Practice

Learning to pray for Israel's destiny—or anything on God's heart—is a process. For that reason each chapter in this book will have a "Target Practice" section with key Scriptures printed out for prayer. I want to encourage you to read through each Scripture and then pray through that passage using the sample italicized prayer that follows.

Scripture and Prayer from Psalm 102:1–2, 13–14

> Hear my prayer, O Lord!
> And let my cry for help come to You.
> Do not hide Your face from me in the day of my distress;
> Incline Your ear to me;
> In the day when I call answer me quickly. . . .
> You will arise and have compassion on Zion;
> For it is time to be gracious to her,
> For the appointed time has come.
> Surely Your servants find pleasure in her stones,
> And feel pity for her dust.

Lord God, we ask that a loud cry would rise up within us, that we would call out to You in a time of distress with confidence knowing that You hear us and answer us quickly. Hear our prayer, O Lord! Thank You for listening to our cries for help. Listen to the cries of Your people, Israel, and give us Your heart of compassion for them. Arise and have compassion on Your people. Hear their prayers, O Lord! Be gracious to Israel, for the time has come. We pray that Your servants would take great pleasure in Israel and have Your heart of compassion for her condition. Give us Your heart, Lord, and let the apple of Your eye become the center of our vision. Amen.

Scripture and Prayer from Psalm 22:4–5

In You our fathers trusted;
  They trusted, and You delivered them.
To You they cried out, and were delivered;
  In You they trusted and were not disappointed.

God, we read in the Bible of Your great faithfulness. When those who trusted in You cried out to You, You delivered each one. We ask, therefore, that the people of Israel would once again put their trust in You, the God of their fathers Abraham, Isaac and Jacob. In the midst of great difficulty, we ask that they would cry out to You and that You would deliver them from all of their troubles. Reveal Yourself to them. Show them again Your great faithfulness and that You are a God who does not disappoint. Amen.

Scripture and Prayer from Isaiah 27:6

In the days to come Jacob will take root,
  Israel will blossom and sprout;
  And they will fill the whole world with fruit.

Thank you, Lord, for Your eternal Word and Your promises to Jacob. Prosper Israel. Let her take root, blossom and sprout. Jesus said that only those who abide in Him will bear much fruit. We ask that Israel will abide in their Messiah so they can bear much, much fruit and that their fruit will fill the whole world. Let the fruit of revival come to Israel, and from Israel to the ends of the Earth. Amen.

Desperate Times Require Desperate Measures!

Let us seize the moment and arise to our destiny: to be watchmen on the walls for Israel's destiny to be fulfilled. Desperate times take desperate measures. Let's not miss the divine opportunity and appointment set before us. Let the prayer army increase in size, purity and effectiveness. This is the time! This is the generation. May a new breed of servant-believers emerge who demonstrate the identity of the Jewish Messiah we serve.

Remember what Jeremiah said: "With weeping they will come, and by supplication I will lead them" (Jeremiah 31:9). I have a challenge for all who are reading this book: Whose supplications will be heard? Who will lift up their voices to fill up a golden bowl in heaven (see Revelation 5:8)? Will you join me?[5] Let The Cry arise! Receive your appointment as a vessel of history, making intercession for such a time as this!

Reflection Questions

1. What does it mean to be a "watchman" in intercession?
2. What scriptural promises remain to be fulfilled for Israel?
3. Give three reasons to pray and take a stand for Israel.

More Study Aids

Goll, Jim W. *Exodus Cry*. Ventura, Calif.: Regal Books, 2001.

Teplinsky, Sandra. *Why Care About Israel?* Grand Rapids, Mich.: Chosen Books, 2004.

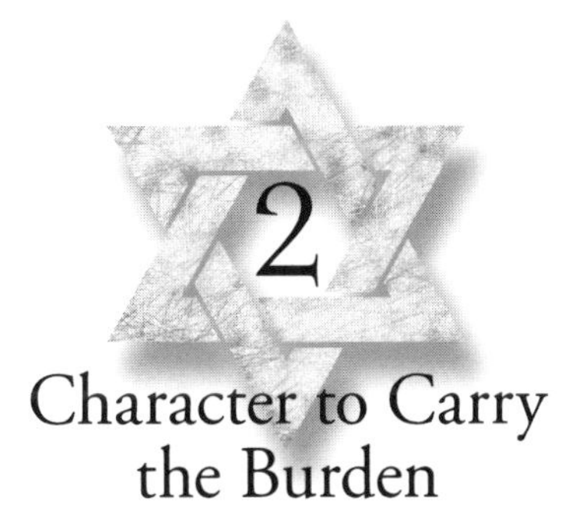

Character to Carry the Burden

"Say to the daughter of Zion,
'Behold your King is coming to you,
Gentle, and mounted on a donkey,
Even on a colt, the foal of a beast of burden.'"

Matthew 21:5

One week before the passion of the cross, Jesus was in need of a burden-bearer who would fulfill prophecy and carry Him into Jerusalem, a city He longed to embrace (see Matthew 21:1–11; 23:37). Jesus therefore called upon a beast of burden—a donkey—to serve His needs. The young donkey made history and is recognized in the liturgical church on Palm Sunday every year as the servant who carried the Messiah. Today Jesus is looking for other beasts of burden to carry His heart for Jerusalem. That is the job description of every serious Israel intercessor.

Strength of character is the ingredient we need to rise to the challenge of carrying the burden of the Lord. The Lord is looking for beasts of burden who can carry Him without taking any of the glory for themselves; vessels who are willing to serve, able to carry the load and to see God's prophetic word come to pass. Are you such a character? Will you be one who fulfills your appointment in history as a burden-bearer for such a time as this?

In the next two chapters, we are going to look at eight people in Scripture who had the character to carry the Lord's heart. I will give you a brief character sketch for each person and then highlight a distinctive strength or passion that enabled him to carry the Lord's burden for his time in history. We are called at such a time as this to take our places in history alongside these eight beasts of burden. Will you join me and these forerunners in carrying God's heart for Israel?

Moses

Moses was a beautiful Hebrew boy born in secret, hidden in a basket in the Nile River and discovered by the daughter of Egypt's ruler. Moses lived in Pharaoh's palace until he was forty years old. When he saw an Egyptian beating a Hebrew, he rose up and killed the attacker but, in the end, fled into the wilderness and took care of sheep for his father-in-law for another forty years.

Moses was taken overnight from an obscure life to national prominence after God appeared to him in blazing fire from the middle of a bush. Moses performed ten of the most dramatic miracles ever recorded in the world's history; miracles that the Jews still commemorate to this day. He led over two million Jews out of Egypt and performed several more amazing miracles that saved his nation from certain destruction.

Moses was God's beast of burden for Israel at the beginning of their history as a nation. He carried Israel out of the bondage of Egypt through the wilderness toward their Promised Land. What kind of character did Moses possess?

Servant for the Glory of the Lord

When Moses came down from Mount Sinai after receiving the Ten Commandments from the Lord, he found Israel worshiping a golden calf and acknowledging it as the god who brought them up from the land of Egypt. Upon hearing God's plan to destroy all the people in punishment, Moses fasted for forty days and nights and cried out to the Lord on Israel's behalf. This fast was immediately following his first fast of forty days while he was on Mount Sinai with the Lord (see Exodus 32; Deuteronomy 9:18).

Moses appealed to the Lord to spare Israel for the sake of His reputation and glory. Moses persisted as he made his appeal to God's covenant nature in keeping the promises He made to Abraham, Isaac and Israel (Jacob). God relented and did not destroy Israel, but He told Moses that He would not go up with them into the Promised Land because He might destroy them on the way. He would send an angel instead to drive out their enemies.

Does that sound to you like a good time to quit pressuring God? Well, Moses did not take the hint. Instead he interceded with even greater desperation on Israel's behalf. Moses understood that God's presence—His glory—was the only thing that distinguished Israel from other nations. He said plainly, "If Your presence does not go with us, do not lead us up from here" (Exodus 33:15). Moses so longed for God's glory during this exchange that he cried out, "I pray You, show me Your glory!" and the Lord did (see Exodus 33:17–34:9).

Did you notice that twice Moses had the opportunity to take the easy way out? First God offered to take the rebellious Israelites off his shoulders—destroy them—and start over with him. Not a bad option unless you like whining, complaining and rebellion. Moses' reply? His hunger for the glory of the Lord compelled him to offer his own life in place of Israel (see Exodus 32:32). Next God offered to send an angel into the land to drive out all their enemies. Again Moses longed for something greater—God's glory. This was a path chosen by someone with character to carry the burden. Oh, to be consumed with the vision of God's glory!

Solomon

Israel was at its most prosperous and most respected during the reign of King Solomon, son of David. But Solomon had humble beginnings. He was the second son of his father's infamous relationship with Bathsheba. When David was very old, Solomon's older half-brother Adonijah held a large, prominent gathering and declared himself king. The Bible says that Adonijah was very handsome and that all Israel expected him to be the next king (see 1 Kings 1:5–25; 2:15). Because of Bathsheba's intervention, however, and because it was the Lord's intention, David appointed Solomon to be his successor.

The Lord appeared in a dream to Solomon early in his reign and said, "Ask what you wish me to give you" (1 Kings 3:5). Solomon acknowledged his inability to lead the nation and humbly requested that God give to him discernment to understand justice. God was pleased with Solomon's response and gave him a wise and discerning heart, unmatched by any other human before or since (see 1 Kings 3:12; 4:29–34).

Solomon led Israel out of a protracted season of war and into an era of peace and prosperity. He "became greater than all the kings of the earth in riches and in wisdom" (1 Kings 10:23) and was God's beast of burden for the nation of Israel at the time of their greatest strength. What kind of character did Solomon possess?

Steward of Wisdom and Wealth

The Bible says that:

> God gave Solomon wisdom and very great discernment and breadth of mind, like the sand that is on the seashore. Solomon's wisdom surpassed the wisdom of all the sons of the east and all the wisdom of Egypt. For he was wiser than all men . . . and his fame was known in all the surrounding nations. He also spoke 3,000 proverbs, and his songs were 1,005. . . . Men came from all peoples to hear the wisdom of Solomon, from all the kings of the earth who had heard of his wisdom.
>
> 1 Kings 4:29–32, 34

When the queen of Sheba heard about the fame of Solomon, she brought a large entourage to Jerusalem to test Solomon with difficult questions. The wisdom of Solomon and the wealth of his kingdom so exceeded the queen's expectations that "there was no spirit in her" (see 1 Kings 10:1–5). The queen praised Solomon:

> How blessed are . . . these your servants who stand before you continually and hear your wisdom. Blessed be the Lord your God who delighted in you to set you on the throne of Israel; because the Lord loved Israel forever, therefore He made you king, to do justice and righteousness.
>
> 1 Kings 10:8–9

The Bible says that "all the earth was seeking the presence of Solomon, to hear his wisdom *which God had put in his heart*" (1 Kings 10:24, emphasis mine). What is most notable about Solomon is not the extravagant wealth or supreme wisdom that he possessed, for these were gifts from God. Solomon's distinctive strength was that he realized that he needed God's wisdom to lead His people successfully in the ways of the Lord, and humbly asked for help in the first place. Solomon also proved to be a faithful steward and willingly shared what

God had given to him with Israel and all who would come to him.

Solomon's character is unparalleled in history. Many today would quickly claim the winning lottery ticket for wisdom and wealth if given the opportunity. Few desire the wisdom with which to fulfill the tasks they have been given by God or are willing to manage what God gives them in order to bring such abundant multiplication for the nation of Israel. Lord, show us our need for Your wisdom and ways!

Nehemiah

After years of exile in Babylon and Persia, about fifty thousand Jews chose in 538 BC to return to Jerusalem and reestablish a Jewish state. Nehemiah was one of thousands of Jews who chose not to return to Judah at first. Instead, he rose to prominence serving in the government's capital city of Susa as the cupbearer to Artaxerxes, king of Persia. When Nehemiah received notice about the sad condition of the people and the city of Jerusalem in 445 BC, he forfeited his position in the Persian court to serve his own nation in the rebuilding of Jerusalem.[1] While Nehemiah's role and influence was in government, his contemporary Ezra was a learned teacher and scribe. Together they brought reformation and restoration to Jerusalem and the Jewish people.

Nehemiah was God's beast of burden to carry Israel through a time of brokenness and battle to a time when the walls of a broken city were restored. What kind of character did Nehemiah possess?

Restorer of Israel's Protection and Godly Living

Three months after Nehemiah received word of the broken condition of the walls around Jerusalem, the weight of his burden showed on his face. The king of Persia said to Nehemiah, "Why is your face sad though you are not sick? This is nothing but sadness of heart" (Nehemiah 2:2). Three months of carrying the burden in prayer and years of faithful service brought a favorable response when the king heard why Nehemiah's countenance was so downcast. The king asked, "What would you request?" (Nehemiah 2:4).

Nehemiah prayed and then made his request to the king, and the king did not just reluctantly answer Nehemiah's request; he was pleased to extend favor to Nehemiah and give him the resources needed to rebuild Jerusalem.

It takes little character to point out a problem. But one who can see the problem, feel compassion and then add strategic action toward restoration possesses the strength of character to carry the burden of the Lord for Israel. Nehemiah was such a person.

Nehemiah investigated what needed to be done, rallied others to work and was confident that they would succeed (see Nehemiah 2:11–20). He organized the labor needed to accomplish the task (see Nehemiah 3). He responded prayerfully and wisely to the substantial opposition that arose (see Nehemiah 4 and 6). Nehemiah made political corrections so that the rulers governed the people fairly (see Nehemiah 5:1–13). In addition, he made many personal sacrifices for the betterment of the people as a whole (see Nehemiah 5:14–19). In the end Nehemiah not only rebuilt the physical wall in Jerusalem but also served to rebuild a spiritual way of life so those who lived in Jerusalem could receive the blessings of God. Is *that* ever needed today—in the land of Israel and every other nation!

With prophetic foresight, Nehemiah viewed the governmental position God granted him as honorable and used his divine favor with the king as an instrument to carry God's burden for Jerusalem's restoration.

Asaph

Asaph was King David's chief musician. He also oversaw others who were assigned by David to minister before the ark of the Lord in making petitions, giving thanks and praising the Lord regularly. Like some of my friends in Nashville, Tennessee, Asaph was a percussion specialist (see 1 Chronicles 16:4–5). Some of the sons of Asaph were set apart for the ministry of prophesying, accompanied by harps, lyres and cymbals (would I like to have been there!). All of them were trained and skilled in music for the Lord (see 1 Chronicles 25:7). These musically talented descendants of Asaph were also mentioned by Ezra and Nehemiah many years later.

Asaph's legacy and life's practice carried on generations after he lived. At the dedication of the wall of Jerusalem under the direction of Ezra and Nehemiah in 444 BC, Israel reinstituted full-time worshipers because they remembered Asaph and his descendants (see Nehemiah 12:44–46). The leaders of the singers, songs of praise and hymns of thanksgiving to God were major players in Israel's transformation back to one nation under the God of their fathers (see Nehemiah 12:27–47).

Asaph was God's beast of burden to demonstrate for Israel's sake the ministry of the "harp and bowl." What kind of character did Asaph and his artistic descendants have?

Pursuer of God's Presence

One of Asaph's songs is recorded in Psalm 73. He tells of a time when he saw the prosperity of the wicked and envied them. Asaph said that his heart was embittered and he was like a "beast" before the Lord (see Psalm 73:22). He cried out to the Lord, "Surely in vain I have kept my heart pure and washed my hands in innocence" (Psalm 73:13). His song then describes how he gained perspective as he went into the house of the Lord. Asaph confesses, "My flesh and my heart may fail, but God is the strength of my heart and my portion forever" (Psalm 73:26). His end resolution was this: "But as for me, the nearness of God is my good; I have made the Lord God my refuge, that I may tell of all Your works" (Psalm 73:28).

The book of Psalms is filled with songs that describe great trouble and the pursuit of God's presence in times of distress and difficulty. The pattern for many of the psalms is something like this: I (or Israel) am in trouble; I want to give up; I go to God; I see who He is; I believe He will help me, and I praise Him for His goodness. Asaph understood this, as did David, Solomon, the sons of Korah, Moses, Joshua, Nehemiah and Ezra. All those called today to the task of the "harp and bowl" also long for the presence of the Lord! Those who carry this musical burden know that God's presence is what makes it possible to carry the weight of life's difficulty and yet see the works of God manifest in the Earth.

Character Must Endure to the End

Character is ultimately tested in the ordinary things of life that each day brings. Character is easy when life's circumstances are easy or when, as with Asaph, God's presence brings clarity and peace to our situations. Character seems difficult to cultivate when your life is shifted and tested, but character only grows as opportunities to call upon greater grace from the Lord arise. It is then we have the opportunity to refine our character with God's strength or fall into the desires of our own flesh.

After decades of enduring the complaining of Israel and interceding on their behalf, Moses was kept from entering the Promised Land because he did not exercise character. Instead he gave in to the desires of his flesh and did not honor the Lord before Israel (see Numbers 20:1–12; Deuteronomy 32:50–52). What a place to fall short of the prize—with the end of the race in sight!

You would think that Solomon's renowned wisdom would have kept him from the foreign women who turned his heart away from the Lord. It did not. His flesh won out over his character in this area, and Solomon passed a weakened inheritance on to his son.

What is my point? Character to carry the burden for your own needs is a daily fight that is only won through prayer and endurance. How much more must we pray and persevere if we are called to carry the burden for Israel. Remember that God's burden is easy and His yoke is light. He does give grace for the journey!

During these past few years, my wife and I have both "walked through the valley of the shadow of death" in battles against cancer. But by grace we came out on the other side knowing even more that the Lord is with us! As for me and my house, we choose the ways of the Lord and continue to cry out for the character needed to be carriers of His glory.

For this chapter's Target Practice, we will pray through some of the prayers that these four history makers prayed during their lifetimes. Their strength of character gave them the grace to cry out on Israel's behalf. But before praying these prayers on Israel's behalf, I invite you to pray with me the following prayer asking for strong character in your own life:

Lord, I want character to carry Your burden.
Like Moses, I want to be a servant for the glory and fame of the Lord.
Like Solomon, I want to be a steward of wisdom and wealth.
Like Nehemiah, I want to be a restorer of Israel's protection and godly practice.
Like Asaph, I want to be a pursuer of Your presence.

Weave these characteristics into my own life
That I may carry the burden for Israel according to Your will for my life.
Strengthen me, Lord; strengthen Your Church,
For Yeshua's sake, and for Israel's sake. Amen.

Target Practice

Let's develop greater character to carry the burden of the Lord by praying the Word of God together. You will soon learn that the main purpose of this book is to get us to prayin'!

Scripture and Prayer from Moses: Numbers 14:17–21

"But now, I pray, let the power of the Lord be great, just as You have declared, 'The Lord is slow to anger and abundant in lovingkindness, forgiving iniquity and transgression; but He will by no means clear the guilty, visiting the iniquity of the fathers on the children to the third and the fourth generations.' Pardon, I pray, the iniquity of this people according to the greatness of Your lovingkindness, just as You also have forgiven this people, from Egypt even until now."

So the Lord said, "I have pardoned them according to your word; but indeed, as I live, all the earth will be filled with the glory of the Lord."

Father, I declare that You are slow to anger and abundant in lovingkindness. You forgive the sins of Your people. Israel is Your inheritance. You have redeemed them by Your great hand. You were the one who brought them out of Egypt and performed many great miracles on their behalf. Remember Your promises to Abraham, Isaac and Jacob. Do not look at the stubbornness of Your people or the wickedness of their sin. Pardon them for Your name's sake. Raise up deliverers of Your people, those who will offer their lives on behalf of Israel and have passion for Your glory and fame. Make the name of Yeshua *known in all the Earth and let all the Earth be filled with Your glory. Amen!*

Scripture and Prayer from Solomon: 1 Kings 8:46–53

When they sin against You (for there is no man who does not sin) and You are angry with them and deliver them to an enemy, so that they take them away captive to the land of the enemy, far off or near; if they take thought in the land where they have been taken captive, and repent and make supplication to You in the land of those who have taken them captive, saying, "We have sinned and have committed iniquity, we have acted wickedly"; if they return to You with all their heart and with all their soul in the land of their enemies who have taken them captive, and pray to You toward their land which You have given to their fathers, the city which You have chosen, and the house which I have built for Your name; then hear their prayer and their supplication in heaven Your dwelling place, and maintain their cause, and forgive Your people who have sinned against You and all their transgressions which they have transgressed against You, and make them objects of compassion before those who have taken them captive, that they may have compassion on them (for they are Your people and Your inheritance which You have brought forth from Egypt, from the midst of the iron furnace), that Your eyes may be open to the supplication of Your servant and to the supplication of Your people Israel, to listen to them whenever they call to You. For You have separated them from all the peoples of the earth as Your inheritance, as You spoke through Moses Your servant, when You brought our fathers forth from Egypt, O Lord God.

Mighty and gracious Father, I call out to You, that the people of Israel would return to You with all their hearts and with all their souls. Hear their prayers and maintain their cause. Forgive Your people who have sinned against You and wipe out all their transgressions which they have transgressed against You. Make them objects of compassion before all the world. Let Your eyes be open to Your people Israel, to listen to them whenever they call to You. I ask this so that Yeshua *would be glorified and that Israel would come into the fullness of her inheritance. Amen.*

Scripture and Prayer from Nehemiah: Nehemiah 1:5–11

I said, "I beseech You, O Lord God of heaven, the great and awesome God, who preserves the covenant and lovingkindness for those who love Him and keep His commandments, let Your ear now be attentive and Your eyes open to hear the prayer of Your servant which I am praying before You now, day and night, on behalf of the sons of Israel Your servants, confessing the sins of the sons of Israel which we have sinned against You; I and my father's house have sinned. We have acted very corruptly against You and have not kept the commandments, nor the statutes, nor the ordinances which You commanded Your servant Moses. Remember the word which You commanded Your servant Moses, saying, 'If you are unfaithful I will scatter you among the peoples; but if you return to Me and keep My commandments and do them, though those of you who have been scattered were in the most remote part of the heavens, I will gather them from there and will bring them to the place where I have chosen to cause My name to dwell.' They are Your servants and Your people whom You redeemed by Your great power and by Your strong hand. O Lord, I beseech You, may Your ear be attentive to the prayer of Your servant and the prayer of Your servants who delight to revere Your name, and make Your servant successful today, and grant him compassion before this man."

Lord, You are a great and awesome God. You preserve the covenant and lovingkindness for those who love You and keep Your commandments. But we have sinned and have been unfaithful to You. Israel has acted corruptly against You and has not kept Your commandments. Cause Your people to return to You and keep Your commandments faithfully. Remember Your promise to gather them from the most remote parts of the Earth and bring them to the place where You have chosen for Your name to dwell. As You did in times of old, show Yourself strong on Israel's behalf and deliver them by Your mighty power. Raise up many Nehemiahs who revere Your name and will use their God-given authority to bring restoration to Jerusalem's brokenness. Grant them compassion before government leaders and make them successful for Your Kingdom's sake. Amen.

Scriptures and Prayer from Asaph: Psalm 44:4–8, 26; 80:2, 18–19

You are my King, O God;
Command victories for Jacob.
Through You we will push back our adversaries;

Through Your name we will trample down those who rise up
against us.
For I will not trust in my bow,
Nor will my sword save me.
But You have saved us from our adversaries,
And You have put to shame those who hate us.
In God we have boasted all day long,
And we will give thanks to Your name forever. . . .
Rise up, be our help,
And redeem us for the sake of Your lovingkindness.

Before Ephraim and Benjamin and Manasseh, stir up Your power
And come to save us! . . .
Then we shall not turn back from You;
Revive us, and we will call upon Your name.
O Lord God of hosts, restore us;
Cause Your face to shine upon us, and we will be saved.

Lord God of Israel, You are the King. Command victories for Israel. Push back their enemies. Trample those who rise up against Your people. I ask that they would not trust in anything of themselves—their own power or wisdom—only in You, the mighty God of Abraham, Isaac and Jacob. Save them from every enemy. Put to shame all those who hate Israel. I pray that You would become Israel's boast and that Your people would give thanks to Your name forever. Rise up and be their help. For the sake of Your lovingkindness, reverse every evil thing the enemy has devised against Your people. Revive Your people so that they call upon Your great name. Restore Your people and cause Your face to shine upon them once again. For Your great name's sake, amen.

Jesus Is Still Looking for a Reliable Beast of Burden

It takes a burden-bearer to carry Jesus where He wants to go. Just as a donkey carried Jesus into Jerusalem on Palm Sunday, Jesus is once again looking for a burden-bearer to carry His heart into Jerusalem, in preparation for His Second Coming. Will you be that beast of burden?

There is good news: All Israel *shall* behold their Messiah, and we can be some of God's little helpers to see this come to pass! God longs to develop in us hearts that beat with His. Let's gaze into the hearts of four more Israel intercessors and see what is needed to be carriers of His presence and thus fulfill His destiny for our lives.

Reflection Questions

1. What does it mean to carry the burden of the Lord?
2. What type of character did Moses exhibit that we need to exemplify?
3. What area of character needs to be developed in your life to be effective in the long term?

More Study Aids

Goll, Jim W. *Kneeling on the Promises*. Grand Rapids, Mich.: Chosen Books, 1999.

Alves, Elizabeth. *Discovering Your Prayer Power*. Ventura, Calif.: Regal Books, 2001.

3 A Heart Like These

> He raised up David to be their king, concerning whom He also testified and said, "I HAVE FOUND DAVID the son of Jesse, A MAN AFTER MY HEART, who will do all My will."
>
> Acts 13:22

The goal of my life is to have a heart like God's as did David, the shepherd boy who became a prophetic psalmist and later a king. Wouldn't it be wonderful to have the Holy Spirit compose a legacy about your life stating that you had a heart like God's? Awesome! I want a passionate heart, one like David's, who by grace followed hard after God. This warrior, prophet, priest and king knew a realm of resiliency in God. He made huge blunders, but he knew the overwhelming love of the Father. You could call him the original "comeback kid"! But David carried more than just a consuming revelation of the lovingkindness of the Lord; he, too, was a beast of burden who carried God's heart for Jerusalem and Israel's sakes. As my friend Mike Bickle has stated for years, "The goal of my life is to be a worshiper of God and a deliverer of men."

Give us all hearts like this, Lord!

As we continue to look at some characters who carried God's heart for Israel's destiny in their generations, please understand that this involves more than just praying accurately or being informed, as important as that is. It takes more than gifting and calling. Those who truly carry Israel through the good times and the bad do so because they have a relationship with the God of Israel. Yes, it takes character to carry the gift. But it also takes a heart like theirs to sustain you in your journey.

Let's proceed now by investigating the lives of four more carriers of God's purposes. Let's glean wisdom from the lives of the four prophets I personally connect with the most: Joel, Isaiah, Jeremiah and Daniel.

Joel

Athaliah was a wicked queen who almost succeeded in wiping out the bloodline of King David and the Messiah. She brutally murdered all the heirs to David's throne except one. She could not find Joash because he was hidden and cared for until age seven, when he was crowned king. He ruled righteously for forty years, repaired the Temple of God and restored worship to the Lord in Jerusalem (see 2 Kings 12). Joel was a prophet who lived during the reign of Joash. Joel prophesied to Jerusalem and to Judah in the south where Solomon's temple and the priests were located.[1] Joel's call was to humility and repentance, because a time of judgment and destruction was near. Joel also spoke a message of hope and salvation to those who would call upon God's name.

Giver of Hope and Light

Upon seeing the devastation of the land, Joel called out from the inner depths of his heart for the people to wail, lament, weep, mourn, cry and grieve. He declared, "Consecrate a fast, proclaim a solemn assembly; gather the elders and all the inhabitants of the land to the house of the Lord your God, and cry out to the Lord" (Joel 1:14). Joel was grieved with what he saw and his immediate response was one of humility, taking the form of fasting, prayer and soberness. That is exactly what the Lord required, as is revealed by His call through Joel for a solemn assembly and repentance: "Return to Me with all your heart, and with fasting, weeping and mourning; and rend your heart and not your garments" (Joel 2:12–13). My point is that Joel himself was first genuinely humble in heart as he was calling out for a heart of humility from the people. Notice what was called for first: "Return to Me with all your heart."

Joel's humility was empowered by his hope in God's character. Joel encouraged the people to "Return to the Lord your God, for He is gracious and compassionate, slow to anger, abounding in lovingkindness and relenting of evil" (Joel 2:13). Joel's hope was not only in God's character but also in God's power on behalf of His people. He prophesied that God would restore all that had been lost; that there would come a time when all Israel would be free from shame, when they would know that God was in the midst of Israel and when He would pour out His Spirit upon all mankind (see Joel 2:21–29). The last words of the book of Joel are words of justice and hope.

This mixture of humility and hope is a mandatory heart characteristic for those who will carry the burden for Israel. Hosea, who lived sixty years after Joel, also prophesied with this harmony. In his call to return to the Lord, Hosea acknowledged that "He has torn us, but He will heal us; He has wounded us, but He will bandage us" (Hosea 6:1). Joel's life demonstrated extreme humility coupled with a hope for complete restoration.

Isaiah

The name *Isaiah* means "Jehovah is salvation." Isaiah, like Joel, called the people and their leaders to repent of their sins against the Lord but also pointed to the salvation that God would bring to His people. Isaiah was a highly educated statesman, knowledgeable in international affairs and familiar with the royal leadership of Judah.[2] The kings who reigned during Isaiah's life included Jotham, Ahaz, Hezekiah and Manasseh (see 2 Kings 15–21).

A stereotypical Old Testament prophet is a person who prophesies pending doom and destruction because of wickedness, like Jonah was told to do over Nineveh. The Bible tells us that Jonah knew of God's heart of mercy but did not want God to be merciful to Nineveh. Isaiah was a very different kind of prophet. The distinctive heart quality that enabled Isaiah to carry the burden for Israel was his understanding of God's mercy and compassion toward Israel and all nations. Isaiah had a revelation that God was a covenant-keeping God and that He would keep the promise He had made to Abraham and his descendants.

Merciful Proclaimer of the Coming Messiah

Of all the prophets in the Old Testament, Isaiah probably had the most complete picture of the coming Messiah. Isaiah prophesied that He would be called Wonderful, Counselor, Mighty God, Eternal Father and Prince of Peace (see Isaiah 9:6). Isaiah also saw the great suffering the Messiah would undergo and described it in Isaiah 53:4–5:

> Surely our griefs He Himself bore,
> And our sorrows He carried. . . .
> He was pierced through for our transgressions,
> He was crushed for our iniquities;
> The chastening for our well-being fell upon Him,
> And by His scourging we are healed.

This revelation of Messiah *Yeshua* and His great sacrifice compelled Isaiah to cry out to God for mercy on Israel's behalf. He declared:

For Zion's sake I will not keep silent,
And for Jerusalem's sake I will not keep quiet,
Until her righteousness goes forth like brightness,
And her salvation like a torch that is burning.
The nations will see your righteousness,
And all kings your glory.

Isaiah 62:1–2

Isaiah saw all the reasons why God should not be merciful, yet because he saw God as Father, he was motivated to cry out for mercy and help. We can see this progression in Isaiah 64:5–9. Isaiah acknowledges Israel's great sin before the Lord in Isaiah 64:5–7. Then Isaiah writes, "But now, O Lord, You are our Father, we are the clay, and You our potter; and all of us are the work of Your hand" (Isaiah 64:8). He then cries out for mercy: "Do not be angry beyond measure, O Lord, nor remember our iniquity forever; behold, look now, all of us are Your people" (Isaiah 64:9).

Let's not model our prayers as much after the heart of the prophet Jonah but rather after the heart of the prophet Isaiah. Isaiah had a heart of mercy because he knew God was a God of mercy who would send the Messiah to redeem all who had gone astray. As God's burden-bearer, Isaiah extended mercy with only a prophetic glimpse of the coming Messiah. How much more can we call out to God for His mercy, because we know the One who is the mediator of a better covenant than the one Isaiah knew (see Hebrews 8:6)?

Jeremiah

Jeremiah grew up in the village of Anathoth, three miles northeast of Jerusalem.[3] At about age twenty, in the thirteenth year of King Josiah's reign (627 BC), he was called by God to prophesy. His contemporaries included Nahum, Zephaniah, Habakkuk, Daniel and Ezekiel.[4] Along with the book of Jeremiah, he also composed the book of Lamentations, a tearful expression of sorrow over the destruction of Jerusalem and the Temple of the Lord. Jeremiah is therefore often referred to as "the weeping prophet."

At times I feel like I am a modern-day Jeremiah. As I get before the Lord's presence, as I get deeper into God's passionate heart for Israel and the Church in the last days, I often just weep—no, *travail*—over the present condition of His people. The Holy Spirit is raising up many "weeping Jeremiahs" in this day—people who have a heart like His.

Weeping Survivor Who Endures to the End

Lamentations 3:49–51, 55–58 says:

> My eyes pour down unceasingly,
> Without stopping,
> Until the Lord looks down
> And sees from heaven.
> My eyes bring pain to my soul
> Because of all the daughters of my city. . . .
> I called on Your name, O Lord,
> Out of the lowest pit.
> You have heard my voice,
> "Do not hide Your ear from my prayer for relief,
> From my cry for help."
> You drew near when I called on You;
> You said, "Do not fear!"
> O Lord, You have pleaded my soul's cause;
> You have redeemed my life.

Jeremiah endured much hardship. He was arrested, beaten, imprisoned, falsely accused, thrown into a cistern where he was left to sink in the mire, nearly put to death and opposed by false prophets. He endured disobedience, rebellion and indifference; observed intimately the conquest and plunder of Jerusalem; and experienced some of the greatest emotional lows that any prophet has ever suffered.[5]

But Jeremiah continued to endure, hear the word of the Lord, faithfully speak to His people and also faithfully appeal to the Lord on Israel's behalf. Jeremiah must have had a strong inner resolve to carry such a heavy assignment for Israel. The kind of hardship and opposition that Jeremiah endured usually ends in anger, bitterness, resentment and a hard heart. Through it all Jeremiah's tears flowed freely over the condition of the people and the land of Israel. Although Jeremiah was angry at Israel's sinful deeds, his heart was still filled with God's compassion for His people.

Lord, give us hearts like this!

Daniel

Daniel was born during the reign of Josiah and was only a teenager when the Babylonians took him as a hostage to Babylon. Nebuchadnezzar had ordered "youths in whom was no defect, who were good-looking, showing intelligence in every branch of wisdom, endowed with understanding and discerning knowledge" to be specially trained for the king's personal service (see Daniel 1:4–5). Daniel fit the description.

God also gave Daniel knowledge and intelligence in every branch of literature and wisdom and understanding of all kinds of visions and dreams. The king found Daniel ten times better in wisdom and understanding than all the magicians and enchanters in his entire kingdom (see Daniel 1:17–20). Daniel proved to be a faithful and excellent servant and for more than sixty years prospered in political leadership under Babylonian and Medo-Persian rulers.[6]

Daniel's excellent spirit allowed him, too, to be a carrier of God's own heart for Israel and to receive prophetic insight for the future even while in captivity to a pagan king.

Man of Excellence and Prophetic Insight

When Darius the Mede took power, he appointed Daniel as one of the top three commissioners to oversee his entire kingdom. The Bible records that:

> Daniel began distinguishing himself among the commissioners and satraps because he possessed an extraordinary spirit, and the king planned to appoint him over the entire kingdom.
>
> Daniel 6:3

The other officials did not like this and "began trying to find a ground of accusation against Daniel . . . but . . . he was faithful, and no negligence or corruption was to be found in him" (Daniel 6:4).

What an incredible testimony! Although Daniel did get set up by these jealous peers and was thrown into a lions' den, God miraculously saved Daniel and he "enjoyed success in the reign of Darius and in the reign of Cyrus the Persian" (Daniel 6:28). Daniel's excellent spirit equipped him to be a beast of burden for Israel by representing the God of Israel to Darius and other influential rulers.

Daniel was studying Jeremiah's writings during the first year of Darius' reign. After reading the word of the Lord given to Jeremiah, Daniel wrote, "So I gave my attention to the Lord God to seek Him by prayer and supplications, with fasting, sackcloth and ashes" (Daniel 9:3). During this time of prayer the angel Gabriel appeared to Daniel to give him insight and understanding about the people of Israel and Jerusalem (see Daniel 9:21–27). God entrusted to Daniel additional prophetic insights about the future, many of which have been accurately fulfilled in history.

Daniel's excellent spirit was tuned in to the prophetic insight of the Lord and enabled him to carry the burden for Israel during a time of captivity. Daniel proved faithful for decades and released prophetic insight to the kings he served, to Israel and to those living many centuries after his life on Earth. This is the cry of my heart: Lord, raise up new Daniels today! Raise up people You can trust to speak the word of the Lord to kings and presidents—those who have excellent spirits and hearts like Yours.

For this chapter's Target Practice, we will pray through some of the prophetic prayers this second group of history makers launched in their lifetimes. The distinctive attributes of their hearts gave them the grace to cry out on Israel's behalf, so before praying the following prayers on Israel's behalf, I encourage you to ask God to grant you a heart like theirs. Then and only then will your own heart be an authentic burden-bearer for Israel's sake.

Lord, I want a heart like these:

Lord, I want grace to carry Your burden.
Like Joel, I want to be a giver of hope and light.
Like Isaiah, I want to be a merciful proclaimer of Messiah's coming.
Like Jeremiah, I want to be a weeping survivor enduring to the end.
Like Daniel, I want to be a person of excellence with prophetic insight.

Weave these attributes into my own heart,
That I, too, can carry the burden for Israel.
Strengthen me, Lord, strengthen the Body of Christ.
For *Yeshua*'s sake, and for Israel's sake,
Give me a heart like these. Amen.

Target Practice

Ready to pray for spiritual understanding and character to match our burden? Then join me now in the following Scripture-based prayers.

Scriptures and Prayer from Joel: Joel 2:12–14, 17, 27; 3:16–18

"Yet even now," declares the LORD,
  "Return to Me with all your heart,
  And with fasting, weeping and mourning;
And rend your heart and not your garments."
  Now return to the LORD your God,
  For He is gracious and compassionate,
  Slow to anger, abounding in lovingkindness,
  And relenting of evil.
Who knows whether He will not turn and relent,
And leave a blessing behind Him,
Even a grain offering and a drink offering
For the LORD your God? . . .
Let the priests, the LORD's ministers,
  Weep between the porch and the altar,
  And let them say, "Spare Your people, O LORD,
  And do not make Your inheritance a reproach,
  A byword among the nations.
  Why should they among the peoples say,
  'Where is their God?'" . . .
"Thus you will know that I am in the midst of Israel,
  And that I am the LORD your God
  And there is no other;
  And My people will never be put to shame."

The LORD roars from Zion
  And utters His voice from Jerusalem,
  And the heavens and the earth tremble.
  But the LORD is a refuge for His people
  And a stronghold to the sons of Israel.
Then you will know that I am the LORD your God,
  Dwelling in Zion, My holy mountain.
  So Jerusalem will be holy,
  And strangers will pass through it no more.
And in that day
  The mountains will drip with sweet wine,
  And the hills will flow with milk,

And all the brooks of Judah will flow with water;
And a spring will go out from the house of the Lord
To water the valley of Shittim.

Gracious Father, I ask that the people of Israel would return to You with all of their hearts. Grant them genuine brokenness of heart and repentance. Reveal Yourself as a God who is gracious and compassionate, slow to anger and abounding in lovingkindness. Spare Your people, O Lord, and do not make Israel, Your inheritance, a reproach among the nations. Remove all shame from Israel. Roar from Zion, O Lord, and let Your voice be heard in Jerusalem. I ask that Israel would know that You are in their midst. Open their eyes to see that You alone are the Lord and there is no other. Be a refuge and a stronghold for Your people. Let them see Your light and hope in the God of their fathers. Thank You that Jerusalem will be holy for Yeshua's *sake. Amen.*

Scriptures and Prayer from Isaiah: Isaiah 63:15–17; 64:1–2, 4–9

Look down from heaven and see from Your holy and glorious habitation;
Where are Your zeal and Your mighty deeds?
The stirrings of Your heart and Your compassion are restrained toward me.
For You are our Father, though Abraham does not know us
And Israel does not recognize us.
You, O Lord, are our Father,
Our Redeemer from of old is Your name.
Why, O Lord, do You cause us to stray from Your ways
And harden our heart from fearing You?
Return for the sake of Your servants, the tribes of Your heritage.

Oh, that You would rend the heavens and come down,
That the mountains might quake at Your presence—
As fire kindles the brushwood, as fire causes water to boil—

To make Your name known to Your adversaries,
That the nations may tremble at Your presence! . . .
For from days of old they have not heard or perceived by ear,
Nor has the eye seen a God besides You,
Who acts in behalf of the one who waits for Him.
You meet him who rejoices in doing righteousness,
Who remembers You in Your ways.
Behold, You were angry, for we sinned,
We continued in them a long time;
And shall we be saved?
For all of us have become like one who is unclean,
And all our righteous deeds are like a filthy garment;
And all of us wither like a leaf,
And our iniquities, like the wind, take us away.
There is no one who calls on Your name,
Who arouses himself to take hold of You;
For You have hidden Your face from us
And have delivered us into the power of our iniquities.
But now, O LORD, You are our Father,
We are the clay, and You our potter;
And all of us are the work of Your hand.
Do not be angry beyond measure, O LORD,
Nor remember iniquity forever;
Behold, look now, all of us are Your people.

Lord God of Israel, You are our Father and You are Israel's Redeemer. Release Your passionate zeal and Your mighty deeds. Let the stirrings of Your heart and Your compassion flow freely toward Israel. Rend the heavens and come down in power. Shake the heavens and make Your name known to Your enemies so that the nations may tremble at Your presence. There is no God like You! Send Your Holy Spirit to arouse Your people so that they can take hold of You. Show Israel Your face and deliver them from the power of their iniquities. I ask that Israel would be a soft clay in Your hands. Have mercy upon Israel, and I ask that others would extend mercy to her as well. For Your great name's sake, amen.

Scriptures and Prayer from Jeremiah: Jeremiah 9:1; 14:8–9; Lamentations 5:19–21

Oh that my head were waters
And my eyes a fountain of tears,
That I might weep day and night
For the slain of the daughter of my people!

O Hope of Israel,
Its Savior in time of distress,
Why are You like a stranger in the land
Or like a traveler who has pitched his tent for the night?
Why are You like a man dismayed,
Like a mighty man who cannot save?
Yet You are in our midst, O Lord,
And we are called by Your name;
Do not forsake us! . . .
You, O Lord, rule forever;
Your throne is from generation to generation.
Why do You forget us forever;
Why do You forsake us so long?
Restore us to You, O Lord, that we may be restored;
Renew our days as of old.

Lord God, Hope of Israel, I ask that tears would flow freely from my eyes over the condition of Israel. I ask that my heart would be filled with compassion, because Israel is in great distress. Be their Savior and their Hope. Be near to Your people and to the city You love. Lord, You rule forever. Your throne is established from generation to generation. Restore Israel completely to Yourself, O Lord. Renew them as in their former days so that You may receive all glory, honor, praise and blessing. Amen!

Scriptures and Prayer from Daniel: Daniel 9:4–6, 9, 15–19

Alas, O Lord, the great and awesome God, who keeps His covenant and lovingkindness for those who love Him and keep His commandments, we have sinned, committed iniquity, acted wickedly and rebelled, even turning aside from Your commandments and ordinances. Moreover, we have not listened to Your servants the prophets, who spoke in Your name to our kings, our princes, our fathers and all the people of the land. . . . To the Lord our God belong compassion and forgiveness, for we have rebelled against Him. . . .

And now, O Lord our God, who have brought Your people out of the land of Egypt with a mighty hand and have made a name for Yourself, as it is this day—we have sinned, we have been wicked. O Lord, in accordance with all Your righteous acts, let now Your anger and Your wrath turn away from Your city Jerusalem, Your holy mountain; for because of our sins and the iniquities of our fathers, Jerusalem and Your people have become a reproach to all those around us. So now, our God, listen to the prayer of Your servant and to his supplications, and for Your sake, O Lord, let Your face shine on Your desolate sanctuary. O my God, incline Your ear and hear! Open Your eyes and see our desolations and the city which is called by Your name; for we are not presenting our supplications before You on account of any merits of our own, but on account of Your great compassion. O Lord, hear! O Lord, forgive! O Lord, listen and take action! For Your own sake, O my God, do not delay, because Your city and Your people are called by Your name.

Lord, You are a great and awesome God, keeping covenant and steadfast love with those who love You and keep Your commandments. I ask that Israel would turn again to Your commandments and listen to Your holy servants. You are full of mercy and forgiveness, even in our rebellion. Make Your name known again through Israel in the same way Your name was known when You brought Your people out of the land of Egypt with a mighty hand. Let Your anger and wrath turn away from Your city, Jerusalem. I ask that Jerusalem would be a praise in the Earth! Lord, let Your face shine brightly upon Your desolated sanctuary. I ask these things because of Your mercies. O Lord, hear; O Lord, forgive; O Lord, listen and take action. Do not delay! For Your own name's sake, O my God, act! Do this because Your city and Your people bear Your name. Amen!

Jesus Is Still Looking for Hearts Like These

We need strong character to carry the burden for Israel and hearts that endure to the end. But—on the flip side of the coin—it is also a blessing and a high privilege to partner with the Holy Spirit in being a watchman on the walls. I consider this one of my greatest joys in life!

Have you volunteered yet? The Holy Spirit is on a mission to find some more beasts of burden for this generation. Join me and Michal Ann and a host of others; sign up for the long haul and ask for a heart full of spiritual wisdom and understanding to carry the presence of God for Israel and the Jewish people. That is it—just sign up by putting your *X* on His dotted line!

Now that we have laid a proper foundation of the character and heart qualities needed to be an effective intercessor and I have (excuse me, He has) you hooked, let's expand our horizons a bit by examining the life of Abraham, the patriarchal prophet and father of faith. Hold on to your hat—I am going to call us to pray for *all* the descendants of Abraham.

Reflection Questions

1. What type of heart must you have to be an effective intercessor for Israel?
2. Jeremiah was known as the weeping prophet. Why?
3. Which of the prophets in this chapter do you identify with the most and why?

More Study Aids

Bickle, Mike. *A Heart Like His*. Lake Mary, Fla.: Charisma House, 2004.

Hess, Tom. *The Watchmen: Being Prepared and Preparing the Way for Messiah*. Washington, D.C.: Progressive Vision International, 1998.

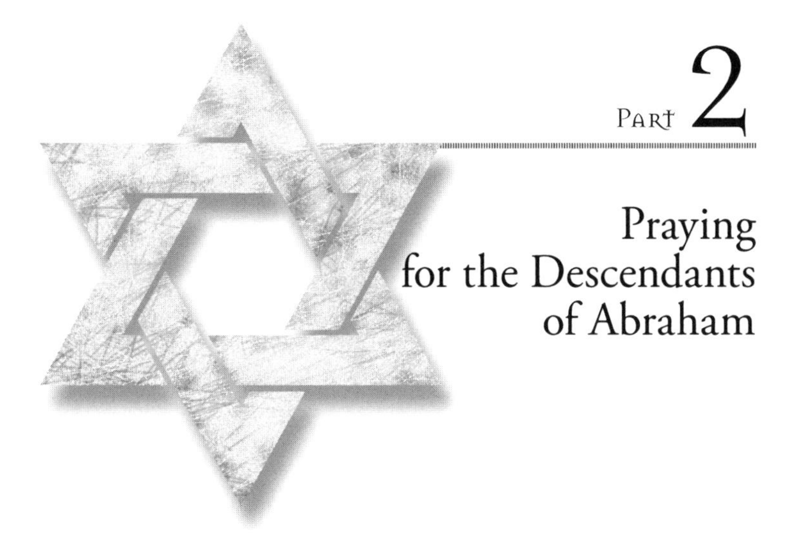

Part 2

Praying for the Descendants of Abraham

4
The Descendants of Hagar

Imagine the scene with me: A teenage lad lay in agony, crying desperately. His mother had laid him under a bush to give him a little reprieve from the scorching heat of the desert. They had no more water—for either their mouths or their souls. The boy's natural father had just turned his back on them and cast them out—suddenly sending them away from the comforts of their home. They were now entirely on their own, left to wander in a wilderness. The mother, not wanting to watch her son wither away and die, sat down a short distance away and began to sob and weep. When everything seemed bleak, then God—yes, God in heaven—heard the lad crying, and He sent supernatural assistance to the boy who would grow up as a strong young man and become the father of a great nation. The boy was Ishmael. His father was Abraham.

In a book about praying for the destiny of Israel, you might expect me to only focus on the Jewish people, the descendants of Abraham, Isaac and Israel (Jacob). But in one of our weekly Israel Prayer Watches, through a visionary experience, the Holy Spirit spoke to me and said, *I am calling you to raise up prayer for the descendants of Abraham. Remember that Ishmael also came from Abraham's seed. In fact, Abraham's seed went into* three *different women.*

The Jews are not the only seed that Abraham produced. In fact there are three different generational lines that comprise Abraham's descendants. Together they all comprise the descendants of Abraham.

We are going to look first of all at the descendants of Hagar. Why am I starting with Hagar? Because Hagar brought forth the firstborn son of Abraham. We will look at the descendants of Abraham in the order in which they were birthed.

God Promises Innumerable Descendants

Abram and Sarai (as they were called before God changed their names) had more than most couples could ask for in terms of wealth, prestige, servants and possessions. But when it came to having what they really wanted, they came up short. Abram and Sarai were barren and, to make matters worse, they were well over normal childbearing age. Michal Ann and I identify with this pain, as we, too, were once barren until the Lord healed us. It must have been quite a surprise to Abram when God took him outside and said, "Now look toward the heavens, and count the stars, if you are able to count them. . . . So shall your descendants be" (Genesis 15:5). Abram believed God against all odds, but after years of waiting for this promise to be fulfilled, he and Sarai took matters into their own hands.

Hagar: Sarai and Abram's Plan of Frustration

One day Sarai came to Abram, probably quite frustrated, and said, "The LORD has prevented me from bearing children. Please go in to my maid; perhaps I will obtain children through her" (Genesis 16:2). Abram listened to his wife, and Sarai's Egyptian maidservant, Hagar, conceived right on the spot. Ouch! That must have stung Sarai pretty badly! As you can imagine, Sarai wished that she had never opened her mouth, ended up despising Hagar and thus treated her harshly. So Hagar felt like an outcast, even though she was not responsible for the decision that led to her pregnancy.

In despair Hagar went out into the wilderness. Genesis 16:7 says, "Now the angel of the LORD found her by a spring of water in the wilderness." What Hagar heard next must have been quite a surprise: "I will greatly multiply your descendants so that they will be too many to count" (Genesis 16:10). So Hagar bore Abram a son and Abram called him Ishmael. "Abraham was eighty-six years old when Hagar bore Ishmael to him" (Genesis 16:16).

Thirteen long years passed. Abram had a teenage son, and Sarai had a despised maid with a son who resembled her husband. Somehow I do not think that those thirteen years were the most pleasant. Abraham was 99 years old when the Lord appeared to him and said:

> "I will establish My covenant between Me and you,
> And I will multiply you exceedingly."
> Abram fell on his face, and God talked with him, saying,
> "As for Me, behold, My covenant is with you,
> And you will be the father of a multitude of nations.
> No longer shall your name be called Abram,
> But your name shall be Abraham;
> For I have made you the father of a multitude of nations.
>
> "I will make you exceedingly fruitful, and I will make nations of you, and kings will come forth from you. I will establish My covenant between Me and you and your descendants after you throughout

their generations for an everlasting covenant, to be God to you and to your descendants after you."

Genesis 17:2–7

After this God instituted the covenant of circumcision with Abraham and his descendants (we'll get back to the initiation of this important covenant in just a moment). What God said next brought Abraham to his knees in laughter.

Then God said to Abraham, "As for Sarai your wife, you shall not call her name Sarai, but Sarah shall be her name. I will bless her, and indeed I will give you a son by her. Then I will bless her, and she shall be a mother of nations; kings of peoples will come from her."

Then Abraham fell on his face and laughed, and said in his heart, "Will a child be born to a man one hundred years old? And will Sarah, who is ninety years old, bear a child?"

Genesis 17:15–17

After enduring decades of barrenness, and then thirteen years of strife and struggle between Sarai and Hagar, Abraham exclaimed, "Oh that Ishmael might live before You!" (Genesis 17:18). Abraham loved Ishmael and wanted him to be blessed. God replied,

No, but Sarah your wife will bear you a son, and you shall call his name Isaac; and I will establish My covenant with him for an everlasting covenant for his descendants after him.

Genesis 17:19

God Promises to Bless Ishmael

God continued to say to Abraham, "As for Ishmael, I have heard you; behold, I will bless him, and will make him fruitful and will multiply him exceedingly." Look closely at what

God said next: "He shall become the father of twelve princes, and I will make him a great nation" (Genesis 17:20). Just like Abraham's grandson Jacob (later renamed Israel), Ishmael would be the father of twelve tribes. God continued, "But My covenant I will establish with Isaac, whom Sarah will bear to you at this season next year" (Genesis 17:21).

Even though God said, "My covenant is established with Isaac," there was a prophetic pronouncement given to Ishmael that we cannot avoid. If we are going to pray properly for Israel, we are going to have to get a wider view of the picture and be able to pray for *all* of the descendants of Abraham. Let's dig a little deeper into Ishmael's role as the firstborn son of Abraham, before Isaac came on the scene.

(By the way, before we get going any further with this line of thought, I want to ask you a question: Have you ever "birthed an Ishmael" in your life? Have you ever experienced the mercy of God while knowing that this was not God's *first* choice? Before we start tossing stones at Sarai, Abram, Hagar and the rest of the company, let's remember that God will cause all things to work together for our good [see Romans 8:28].)

Who was the first person to receive God's covenant of circumcision? This may surprise you, but it was not Abraham or Isaac. Genesis 17:25 says, "And Ishmael his son was thirteen years old." Ishmael was half Hebrew because he came from Abraham's seed. Abraham was a Moabite-Hebrew. The term "Jew" wasn't even in existence yet. The word *Jew*, or *Jewish*, is taken from the tribe of Judah, the fourth of twelve sons born to Israel, from whom the twelve tribes of Israel originated. But who was the first to be circumcised? My goodness, it was Ishmael! Abraham was circumcised on the same day, at 99 years old (see Genesis 17:26), but Ishmael was only thirteen when "he was circumcised in the flesh of his foreskin."

Circumcision is not a big deal to the Western world. It is simply a medical health procedure performed on newborn baby boys. But the Bible looks at circumcision as an external sign of a covenant being kept between God and His people. The apostle Paul in his letter to the Galatians (and also in Romans) speaks extensively about the spiritual symbolism contained in this physical act God commanded Abraham to perform.

I opened this chapter with the story of Hagar and Ishmael being sent away by Abraham. Abraham had made a great feast on the day that Isaac was weaned. But Sarah saw Ishmael mocking Isaac and did not like it. She said to Abraham, "Drive out this maid and her son, for the son of this maid shall not be an heir with my son Isaac" (Genesis 21:10). There was a reason she responded as she did; one man, two women and two sons is not a proven combination for harmony.

Abraham was greatly unsettled because he cared for Ishmael, a son born of his own flesh. God exhorted Abraham, "Do not be distressed because of the lad and your maid [Hagar]; whatever Sarah tells you, listen to her, for through Isaac your descendants shall be named." God continued, "And of the son of the maid I will make a nation also, because he is your descendant" (Genesis 21:12–13).

Wow! What a demonstration of God's faithfulness to Abraham, even though Ishmael was a by-product of the flesh trying to work out God's promises. Because Ishmael was Abraham's descendant, God promised to bless him.

Torn, yet comforted by these words,

> Abraham rose early in the morning and took bread and a skin of water and gave them to Hagar, putting them on her shoulder, and gave her the boy, and sent her away. And she departed and wandered about in the wilderness at Beersheba.
>
> Genesis 21:14

As Hagar sat a distance away from her son, who was thirsty and crying, the angel of the Lord appeared to Hagar a second time. In their first encounter, while she was a pregnant runaway, the angel had declared to her, "I will greatly multiply your descendants so that they will be too many to count" (Genesis 16:10). Now the angel of the Lord affirmed her son again: "I will make a great nation of him" (Genesis 21:18). God miraculously provided water for Hagar and Ishmael, and they survived. Genesis 21:20 says, "God was with the lad, and he grew."

What did that say? "God was with the lad!" This was another demonstration of God's divine mercy, blessing the mess that Abraham and Sarah created.

Hagar was an Egyptian (see Genesis 16:1), so the fruit that first came from Abraham was half Egyptian and half Moabite-Hebrew. Hagar took a wife for Ishmael from the land of Egypt. From Ishmael came twelve princes, twelve tribes, a great nation. The Bible says so, three times it is declared. This great nation descended from Ishmael is the Arab people.

Through Abraham, All Nations Will Be Blessed

Let's look at Abram's first encounter with the Lord just after his father, Terah, died. The Lord made it very clear from the start that *all* who would come from Abraham would be blessed. Genesis 12:1–3 says:

> Now the Lord said to Abram,
> "Go forth from your country,
> And from your relatives
> And from your father's house,
> To the land which I will show you;
> And I will make you a great nation,
> And I will bless you,
> And make your name great;
> And so you shall be a blessing;
> And I will bless those who bless you,
> And the one who curses you I will curse.
> And in you all the families of the earth will be blessed."

Let me repeat that again: through Abram *all* the families of the Earth will be blessed. All! This includes the descendants of Ishmael—the Arab people. Or do you think that God was unaware of who that "all" would include?

Let's skip ahead 24 years to Abram's commissioning, found in Genesis 17:1–14. We have already looked at this passage, but I want to highlight again God's promise to establish His covenant with all of Abram's descendants, not just one particular generational line. God promised the following to *Abraham*, which means "father of a multitude":

> I will establish My covenant between Me and you and your descendants after you throughout their generations for an everlasting covenant, to be God to you and to your descendants after you.
>
> Genesis 17:7

The apostle Paul emphasized that God "made from one man, every nation of mankind to live on all the face of the earth, having determined their appointed times and the boundaries of their habitation, that they would seek God" (Acts 17:26–27).

Jesus said that "God so loved—" who? Just those who love Him? Just Israel? Just believers in Jesus Christ? No, God so loved the *world* (see John 3:16)! Jesus came to make a way to the Father for all nations, a way for all the peoples of the Earth to be blessed through the covenant God made with Abraham.

The Arabs Are Not the Enemy!

I want to make an appeal, and it is an appeal that I have a right to make, because I have been an Israel intercessor for decades. I am going to make an appeal to other Israel intercessors. My appeal is this: Do not call the Arabs our enemy. Do not treat the Arabs as if they were our enemy, because Paul made it very clear in his letter to the Ephesians that we do not wrestle against people (see Ephesians 6:12).

Let me say it a bit more boldly: *The Palestinians are not our enemy!* We do not wrestle against flesh and blood. We wrestle against powers, principalities and spirits of wickedness in the heavenly places, which do operate through people. But we do not wrestle against people. We wrestle against powers of darkness.

We must constantly keep proper biblical perspective or we will get into a wrong kind of romanticism concerning Israel. Israel is undoubtedly the apple of God's eye, but that does not make Ishmael the hated enemy. You do not have to hate the Arabs to love Israel. You can and should love both peoples.

I have a dear American friend named Rick Ridings. Rick and his wife, Patti, are prophetic, intercessory-missionary statesmen who, after years of service in Belgium, now live with their family in Jerusalem. Rick aptly states: "If you love the Jews with a soulish love, you will hate the Arabs. If you love the Arabs with a soulish love, you will hate the Jews. But if you love either people (Jews or Arabs) with God's heart, then you will authentically love the others."

God made a covenant with Abraham, Isaac and Jacob. Jacob wrestled with the angel of the Lord, his nature changed and he became Israel. God confirmed His covenant with both the descendants of Abraham and the seed of Abraham. When we are speaking about this enduring covenant, you see, there is a difference between the plural word *descendants* and the singular word *seed*.

The apostle Paul talks about the *seed*, singular (see Galatians 3:16), saying that Jesus the Messiah is the one seed. Paul goes on to say, "If you belong to Christ, then you are Abraham's descendants, heirs according to the promise" (Galatians 3:29). This seed comes for us through a covenant line of faith, not soul and flesh. The original commission that was given to Abraham is, in a sense, the same commission that is later given to the Church: "Go therefore and make disciples of all the nations" (Matthew 28:19). These are the same nations that God promised would be blessed through Abraham's seed.

One blessing does not nullify the other! Both the spiritual descendants of Abraham and the physical descendants of Abraham are valid recipients of God's grace. We are not in competition!

The Prophetic Destiny of Ishmael

Let's look at Genesis 25:12: "Now these are the records of the generations of Ishmael, Abraham's son." (This becomes important if we are going to pray for the descendants of Abraham.) Now we are going to see some of Abraham's grandchildren.

God's word to Abraham about twelve princes coming from Ishmael came to pass (see Genesis 25:16)! The next few verses give us the names of the twelve sons of Ishmael, but we will only look at the first two—Nebaioth the firstborn and Kedar.

One fact to note for future reference is where Ishmael's descendants settled. Look at Genesis 25:18: "They settled from Havilah to Shur which is east of Egypt as one goes toward Assyria." Remember *Assyria*.

Now let's move forward to Isaiah 60:7. Isaiah prophesied, "All the flocks of Kedar—"

Where did we here about Kedar? Who is Kedar? He was the second son of Ishmael!

"—All the flocks of Kedar will be gathered together to you, the rams of Nebaioth—"

Where did Nebaioth come from? He was the firstborn son of Ishmael!

> All the flocks of Kedar will be gathered together to you,
> The rams of Nebaioth will minister to you;
> They will go up with acceptance on My altar,
> And I shall glorify My glorious house.

We see here that the descendants of Ishmael—the Arab people—are going to be acceptable before God. They are going to end up glorifying God, and there will be an altar of worship that is going to come out of Ishmael's seed. Amazing indeed!

This could really mess up some of our narrow thinking, though! Let me simply state: *There is a whole lot of prophecy yet to be fulfilled on planet Earth.* God has an enormous heart and He has plans for all peoples.

Isaiah 60:1–3 declares:

> Arise, shine; for your light has come,
> And the glory of the Lord has risen upon you.
> For behold, darkness will cover the earth
> And deep darkness the peoples;
> But the Lord will rise upon you,
> And His glory will appear upon you.
> Nations will come to your light,
> And kings to the brightness of your rising.

This sounds very similar to the words God spoke to Abraham in Genesis 12 and 17!

Target Practice

Now that our understanding has been expanded, let's have some Scripture-based Target Practice!

Scriptures and Prayer from Genesis 12:2–3; Isaiah 60:7

> And I will make you a great nation,
> And I will bless you,
> And make your name great;
> And so you shall be a blessing;
> And I will bless those who bless you,
> And the one who curses you I will curse.
> And in you all the families of the earth will be blessed.

> All the flocks of Kedar will be gathered together to you,
> The rams of Nebaioth will minister to you;

They will go up with acceptance on My altar,
And I shall glorify My glorious house.

Father God, You have made Abraham a great nation. His descendants are indeed uncountable. You said that You would bless those who bless and curse those who curse. Forgive us for cursing the descendants of Your son Ishmael. I ask that You would bless the Arab people. Make them a blessing to the nations of the Earth. Gather them to Yourself and use them to bless Israel. I ask that they would minister to Israel instead of destroying her. May they glorify Your house and be acceptable in Your sight for the sake of Your Son, Yeshua. *Amen.*

Scripture and Prayer from Acts 17:26–27

[God] made from one man every nation of mankind to live on all the face of the earth, having determined their appointed times and the boundaries of their habitation, that they would seek God, if perhaps they might grope for Him and find Him, though He is not far from each one of us.

Father God, You fashioned Ishmael in Hagar's womb and You determined his appointed times and where he would live. You are not far from Ishmael's descendants. Your Word says that You are near to all who call upon You. I ask that the Arab people would seek You, call out to You and find You to be their very present hope in trouble. Deliver them from evil and direct them into paths of righteousness for Your name's sake. Amen.

Scripture and Prayer from 2 Peter 3:9

The Lord is not slow about His promise, as some count slowness, but is patient toward you, not wishing for any to perish but for all to come to repentance.

Heavenly Father, thank You that You will fulfill every promise that You gave to Abraham. Thank You also for Your patience with us. Help us to think correctly concerning the Arab people. Forgive us for judging the descendants of Ishmael instead of interceding on their behalf. You do not wish for them to perish but for all of them to come to repentance. I ask that godly sorrow and Your kindness would draw the Arab people to repentance and faith in the one true God, Yeshua. *Send a mighty outpouring of Your Spirit among the descendants of Ishmael for Jesus Christ's sake. Amen.*

Reaching for the Destiny of Ishmael

Let's not write off the whole Islamic issue as a lost cause. I declare that the Islamic veil shall be pierced! A great harvest is at hand! Friend and author Sandra Teplinsky emphasizes this point in her balanced and insightful book *Why Care about Israel?*:

> From God's perspective, it is harvest time for Arab Muslim souls, though a stiff price will likely be paid for it. Amid the world's war on terror, expect to see masses of converted Arabs and prepare to undergird them sacrificially. Remember that for the patriarch's sake they, too, are uniquely loved.[1]

In closing let me recite to you the poignant words of a Jewish scholar of scholars and a believer in the land of Israel today. Listen to the words of Avner Boskey of Final Frontier Ministries:

> The [Bible's] prophetic word has shaped much of the destiny of the greater Arab nation and its relationship with the world. Fierce independence, a wild and untamable soul, and arrogant animosity can characterize Arab dealings (at their worst) with the world. But the Arab world at its best manifests freedom of abandoned worship, generosity, graciousness and sacrificial zeal. When Messiah Jesus is allowed to transform their hearts, the descendants of Ishmael will find God bringing sweet out of the bitter, and they will discover the beauty of their Abrahamic connection in a totally new way.

> Peace and cooperation will supplant wildness and strife, and love between Arab and Jewish cousins will bloom again.[2]

Let's pierce the veil of Islam through the power of the Gospel of the Kingdom and call forth the fulfillment of God's great promise. Why not? God has, after all, promised in the book of Revelation that there will be before His throne a people of every tongue, of every tribe, of every kindred and of every nation. Therefore let us reach into the heart of God for the prophetic destiny of the tribe of the twelve princes of Ishmael, and speak life rather than death!

Now take a quick breath before we turn our attention to the descendants of Abraham that came through Sarah!

Reflection Questions

1. Who are the descendants of Hagar today?
2. What prophetic promise is mentioned in Scripture for the descendants of Hagar?
3. In what way can you pray God's destiny for the Arab peoples across the Middle East today?

More Study Aids

Boskey, Avner. *A Perspective on Islam*. Nashville, Tenn.: Final Frontier Ministries, 2001.

Brimmer, Rebecca J. *"For Zion's Sake I Will Not Be Silent."* Jerusalem, Israel: Bridges for Peace International, 2003.

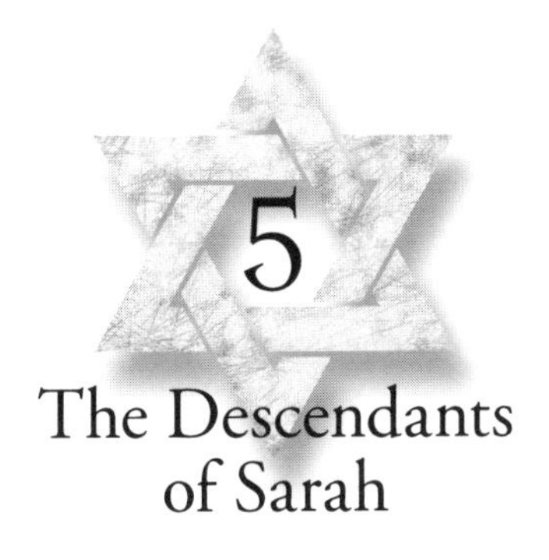

5 The Descendants of Sarah

> This is what the LORD Almighty says: "In those days ten men from all languages and nations will take firm hold of one Jew by the hem of his robe and say, 'Let us go with you, because we have heard that God is with you.' "
>
> Zechariah 8:23, NIV

Thirteen years after the birth of Ishmael, God appeared to 99-year-old Abram and said, "I am God Almighty" (Genesis 17:1). This is the first time in Scripture that God reveals Himself as "God Almighty" or, in Hebrew, *El Shaddai*, which means "All-Sufficient One." The Hebrew word *shad* is always translated as "breast." In the same way a mother provides all that is sufficient for her newborn's nourishment, God was about to reveal to Abram that He is all-powerful and able to satisfy with "blessings of the breasts and of the womb" (Genesis 49:25). This is also the way God chose to reveal Himself to Isaac, Jacob, Joseph, Moses and many others. It is the way that we must see God if we are to intercede on behalf of the descendants of Sarah.

God Provides a Miracle Child

Let's look again at what God initially promised to the father of faith, Abram:

> "I will establish My covenant between Me and you,
> And I will multiply you exceedingly."
> Abram fell on his face, and God talked with him, saying,
> "As for Me, behold, My covenant is with you,
> And you will be the father of a multitude of nations.
> No longer shall your name be called Abram,
> But your name shall be Abraham;
> For I have made you the father of a multitude of nations.
>
> "I will make you exceedingly fruitful, and I will make nations of you, and kings will come forth from you. I will establish My covenant between Me and you and your descendants after you throughout their generations for an everlasting covenant, to be God to you and to your descendants after you."
>
> Genesis 17:2–7

Then God had a surprise for Abraham. He said:

> "As for Sarai your wife, you shall not call her name Sarai, but Sarah shall be her name. I will bless her, and indeed I will give you a son by her. Then I will bless her, and she shall be a mother of nations; kings of peoples will come from her." Then Abraham fell on his face and laughed, and said in his heart, "Will a child be born to a man one hundred years old? And will Sarah, who is ninety years old, bear a child?"
>
> Genesis 17:15–17

God reassured Abraham that it was not Ishmael who would fulfill His promise of a child from his own body. He said:

> Sarah your wife will bear you a son, and you shall call his name Isaac [which means "he laughs"]; and I will establish My covenant with him for an everlasting covenant for his descendants after him. . . . My covenant I will establish with Isaac, whom Sarah will bear to you at this season next year.
>
> Genesis 17:19, 21

The Lord visited Abraham again, shortly after this exchange. As Abraham was sitting at the tent door in the heat of the day, three men appeared, standing opposite him. He greeted them quickly and asked them to stay and rest with him. After receiving the food Abraham prepared for them to eat, the Lord said to him, "I will surely return to you at this time next year; and behold, Sarah your wife will have a son." (See Genesis 18:1–10.)

Sarah was listening nearby at the tent door, and the Bible records that:

> Sarah laughed to herself, saying, "After I have become old, shall I have pleasure, my lord [Abraham] being old also?" And the LORD said to Abraham, "Why did Sarah laugh? . . . Is anything too difficult for the LORD? At the appointed time I will return to you, at this time next year, and Sarah will have a son." Sarah denied it however, saying, "I did not laugh"; for she was afraid. And He said, "No, but you did laugh."
>
> Genesis 18:12–15

Abraham and Sarah were old, advanced in age. Sarah was way past a normal woman's ability to have a child. But God decided that they were not too old to receive a very special gift.

Laughter Is Born as the Promise Comes Forth

Genesis 21 says:

> Then the Lord took note of Sarah as He had said, and the Lord did for Sarah as He had promised. So Sarah conceived and bore a son to Abraham in his old age, at the appointed time of which God had spoken to him. Abraham called the name of his son who was born to him, whom Sarah bore to him, Isaac. Then Abraham circumcised his son Isaac when he was eight days old, as God had commanded him. Now Abraham was one hundred years old when his son Isaac was born to him. Sarah said, "God has made laughter for me; everyone who hears will laugh with me." And she said, "Who would have said to Abraham that Sarah would nurse children? Yet I have borne him a son in his old age."
>
> Genesis 21:1–7

It seems as though the Lord derived great enjoyment from this whole affair! Abraham laughed and Sarah laughed, but I guess you could say that God had the last laugh on the matter, because Isaac's name means "he laughs." Isn't that amazing!

What a joyful moment for Sarah and Abraham! This was the birth of the promised child of faith; not another fleshly, frustration-motivated attempt to bring the promise to pass. Abraham circumcised Isaac when he was eight days old, as God had commanded him. The number eight was used in Scripture to signify a time of new beginning. This new beginning was conceived when Abram had faith for the impossible (having descendants as numerous as the stars), and birthed as "laughter" when the promise was revealed.

In the same way we, too, must have faith for what we see as impossible for the nation of Israel, fully confident that our joy will be made full when the impossible comes to pass. I have undaunted faith when it comes to the promises of God concerning the descendants of Sarah—want to join me?

The Descendants of Sarah

Who are the descendants of Sarah? What does this phrase mean? Isaac was the only child that Abraham and Sarah had through their union. He in turn married the beautiful maiden Rebekah. "Then Isaac brought her into his mother Sarah's tent, and he took Rebekah, and she became his wife, and he loved her; thus Isaac was comforted after his mother's death" (Genesis 24:67).

"Isaac prayed to the Lord on behalf of his wife, because she was barren; and the Lord answered him and Rebekah his wife conceived" (Genesis 25:21). As you probably know, Rebekah brought forth a pair of struggling twin boys named Esau and Jacob. As time passed Jacob, with the help of his mother, treacherously stole the blessing of the firstborn son away from Esau. Jacob, the heel-grabber and supplanter, fled with the blessing, which could not be revoked.

Jacob met and became dazzled by Rachel, arranged to marry her and, in turn, was deceived by Laban, her father. It is forever true that what a man sows he also reaps! Jacob was given Leah, the older and weak-eyed daughter, instead of Rachel as a surprise in his tent on his wedding night! But seven days later Jacob got his wish, receiving Rachel also as his much-sought-after bride, although he had to work another seven years for her (see Genesis 29).

Leah had no problem bearing sons for Jacob, and this caused jealousy and desperation to arise in Rachel. "Now when Rachel saw that she bore Jacob no children, she became jealous of her sister; and she said to Jacob, 'Give me children, or else I die'" (Genesis 30:1).

The competition was now on! Many trials, errors and woes beset Rachel until, finally,

> God remembered Rachel, and God gave heed to her and opened her womb. So she conceived and bore a son and said, "God has

> taken away my reproach." She named him Joseph, saying, "May the Lord give me another son."
>
> Genesis 30:22–24

As the saga unfolded, Jacob had a heavenly encounter and wrestled with the angel of the Lord throughout the night. Jacob prevailed in this wrestling match, received a blessing and his name was changed from *Jacob*, "the deceiver," to *Israel.*

> The identity *Israel* is given initially to Abraham's grandson Jacob. In his unredeemed nature, Jacob does not always behave honorably, scheming and deceiving his older brother Esau out of his birthright. When Esau seeks revenge, Jacob flees for his life. Frankly, the young man strikes us as an unlikely candidate for *Yahweh's* everlasting favor.[1]

Yes, Jacob wrestled with the Lord and won! You heard me correctly. It is my persuasion, however, that the Lord let Jacob *think* he won, just like He does with you and me. The Lord was, in reality, the one who won out; Jacob's nature was changed, and he walked with a limp from that day forward. The name *Israel* means:

> "To strive, persist or exert oneself." Second, *Yisrael* stands for "prince with God," from a play on the Hebrew words *sar* meaning "prince" and *El.* Combining both meanings, we could say that *Yisrael* is a prince who has striven with God and men, and overcome (see Genesis 32:28).[2]

Now Israel, like Ishmael, the son of Hagar, became the father of many sons. Twelve tribes emerge from his lineage (see Genesis 30:1–24; 35:16–18). Prophetic interpretation tells us that twelve is the number of governmental authority. Jesus, for example, choose twelve disciples. Israel brought forth twelve full tribes, and these became the descendants of Abraham and Sarah who inherited the covenant promises of God.

One of these twelve sons of Jacob was named Judah, meaning "thanks" or "praise." The Messiah Himself is known as the Lion from the tribe of Judah (see Revelation 5:5). It is from the name Judah that the term *Jew* has derived.

> The word Jew comes from Judah, one of Jacob's twelve sons and progenitor of the tribe of Judah (into which Yeshua was born). . . . The connotation is that the Jews are a people created for God's praise.[3]

God's Covenant Plan

I, like many of you, have been seeking answers for some time. I remember the days of hearing international Bible teacher Derek Prince logically reason through the minefield of questions surrounding subjects like "Who is Israel?" and "The Role of the Church and Israel in the Last Days." This beloved pioneer related some of his own pilgrimage in his book *Promised Land*:

> The first eleven chapters of the Bible, I realized, serve as an introduction. They fill in the background and set the stage for all that is to follow. From then on, the Bible is essentially the history of Abraham and the nation descended from him through Isaac and Jacob—that is to say, Israel.
>
> There was, I discovered, a distinction to be made between the words *Israel* and *Israelite*, and the words *Jew* and *Jewish*. Linguistically, *Jew* is derived from *Judah*, the name of one of the twelve tribes of Israel.
>
> From the time of the Babylonian captivity, however, all the Israelites who returned to the land of Israel were called Jews, irrespective of their tribal background. This usage is carried over into the New Testament. Paul, for example, was from the tribe of Benjamin; yet he called himself a Jew (see Acts 21:39).
>
> In contemporary usage, these four words are not fully interchangeable. Israel and Israelite focus primarily on national origin and background. Jew and Jewish focus more on religion, culture

> and later history. Since the birth of the state of Israel in 1948, the word Israelite has been added, referring to any citizen of the state, whether of Jewish, Arab or Druse descent. One unique feature of the history of Israel, as recorded in the Bible, is that part of it was written in advance of the events, as prophecy. Taken together, the historical and prophetic portions of the Bible constitute a complete history of the people of Israel.[4]

God's covenant with Israel is one of the oldest legal contracts in history. He made the covenant with Abraham and then passed it on to Isaac. The generational blessing proceeded on to Jacob, whose name was changed to Israel. As Jacob's life was transformed, he passed the torch on to his clan of twelve, who inherited the promise. The "Jews" as a unique people of faith came into existence then, and the covenant plan of God was secured. More than three thousand years after it was enacted with Abraham, this covenant contract is still in force today.

The specifics of this contract are laid out in Scripture for all to read. Unlike human contracts, which have time limitations, God's covenant promises are tied to His nature of faithfulness, mercy and love. His plans are eternal—without end—and God's covenant with Abraham was unconditional.

It is, therefore, ultimately God who will keep His word and see that it comes to pass. I agree with Jeremiah: "Great is His faithfulness." God will keep His covenant promises simply because He said that He would do so, and you can take God at His word! The descendants of Sarah are the keepers of the covenant purposes and plans of God.

First Priority—Land or People or What?

I am sure that I have already rattled the cages of many readers. While I am at it, I guess I might just as well go for the jugular! What is most important in the heart of God—the land of Israel or the people of Israel?

To some people, due to either a wrong emphasis or a flat-out misconception, the answer seems to be "the land." But if that is your answer, then you have just failed the test. Though there is a "land covenant" with the descendants of Sarah, which is extremely important in the ways and purposes of the Holy Spirit, it is forever settled in God's heart that the "land of the heart" takes priority.

How should intercessors for Israel pray into the quagmire that is the Middle East? Asher Intrater, a Messianic scholar and Rabbi who lives in Israel, explains clearly and forcefully:

> All of the land in Israel belongs, by divine covenant, to the Jewish people. Claims of the Islamic world of ownership of the land of Israel are a direct rebellion and challenge to the Word of God.[5]

Asher continues:

> I agree with the most radical proponents of total land possession for Israel. However, land possession is not the ONLY issue involved. When you stress one issue to the lack of others, you can make a mistake, even when what you are saying is right. There are other issues in Israel, such as the moral collapse in schools . . . unemployment, violence, mental and emotional traumas and on and on. Caring for these issues must also be on the agenda.[6]

This fiery, energetic voice crying in the wilderness delivers the knockout punch when he, as a Jew of Jews, states:

> Most of all, there is the issue of evangelism. Praying for the land without praying for Israel's salvation accentuates only one aspect of God's purposes for Israel. When evangelism is avoided, then other issues get a bigger share of the emphasis than what is due.[7]

In 1882, Joseph Rabinowitz, a prominent Jewish leader in Kishniv, made a journey to Palestine (as it was called then). He was sent officially by his orthodox Jewish community, representing like-minded Jews who were determined to see if

Palestine was the right place to establish a Jewish homeland. Rabinowitz visited the Mount of Olives during his brief stay. He sat on a slope near Gethsemane just as the sun was setting, and became troubled on the inside.

> A passage from the Hebrew New Testament he had read 15 years earlier flashed in his mind: "So if the Son makes you free, you will be free indeed" (John 8:36). In that moment, he began to realize that Jesus was the King and Messiah, the only one who could save Israel. . . . When Rabinowitz returned home, he studied the Hebrew New Testament. . . . He did not claim to know if the land of Palestine was the hope of the Jewish people. Then, touching his chest, he would say, "This is the land, the land of the heart. It is what God wants us to obtain." He would sometimes add, "The key to the Holy Land lies in the hands of our brother, Jesus."[8]

Joseph Rabinowitz was a forerunner statesman who, like Jeremiah of old, cried out that our hearts of stone would be changed into hearts of flesh. In our day, thousands of the Jewish descendants of Abraham, Isaac and Israel have placed their faith in *Yeshua* as their Messiah. A worldwide Messianic movement of Hebrew-Christian congregations has sprung forth as the eyes of Jewish people have been opened to behold their glorious Messiah.

May many sons and daughters of Sarah arise and take their rightful place in leading the processional of praise before the majesty of the one true God![9]

Target Practice

Want to pray now? It's time! Once again let's practice a prayer session together using Scripture-based prayers, this time for the descendants of Sarah—the Jewish people. Yes, let's intercede for both the nation of Israel and for the Jewish people yet scattered worldwide. I am excited! Are you ready to make Kingdom impact?

Scriptures and Prayer from Genesis 21:1–3; Isaiah 35:10; 46:3–4

Then the Lord took note of Sarah as He had said, and the Lord did for Sarah as He had promised. So Sarah conceived and bore a son to Abraham in his old age, at the appointed time of which God had spoken to him. Abraham called the name of his son who was born to him, whom Sarah bore to him, Isaac.

And the ransomed of the Lord will return
And come with joyful shouting to Zion,
With everlasting joy upon their heads.
They will find gladness and joy,
And sorrow and sighing will flee away.

Listen to Me, O house of Jacob,
And all the remnant of the house of Israel,
You who have been borne by Me from birth
And have been carried from the womb;
Even to your old age I will be the same,
And even to your graying years I will bear you!
I have done it, and I will carry you;
And I will bear you and I will deliver you.

Gracious Father, take note of Your people, Israel, and do for them as You have promised. Against all odds, may Israel give birth at the appointed time to laughter and joy. Thank You that the redeemed of the Lord will return with joyful shouting to Israel, and they will have everlasting joy and gladness. You are El Shaddai—*All-Sufficient One—who completely provides and satisfies His children. Continue to carry Your people, bear them up and deliver them for their Messiah's sake, until He returns for His own. Amen.*

Scripture and Prayer from Romans 11:25–27

For I do not want you, brethren, to be uninformed of this mystery—so that you will not be wise in your own estimation—that a partial hardening has happened to Israel until the fullness of the

Gentiles has come in; and so all Israel will be saved; just as it is written,

> "THE DELIVERER WILL COME FROM ZION,
> HE WILL REMOVE UNGODLINESS FROM JACOB.
> THIS IS MY COVENANT WITH THEM,
> WHEN I TAKE AWAY THEIR SINS."

Father God, I ask that we would not be wise in our own eyes, but that we would understand the mystery of Israel. Thank You for extending Your mercy and grace to the Gentiles by allowing them [me] to be grafted into the richness of Your tree of life. Cause the Church to fulfill her commission, to preach the Gospel to the whole world, so that the full number of Gentiles will come into the Kingdom and salvation will come to all of Israel. I ask that You would come and deliver the Jews—Your natural branches—and remove all ungodliness from Israel. Take away their sins and restore them to Yourself for Your great name's sake. Amen.

Scripture and Prayer from Isaiah 60:1–2

> Arise, shine; for your light has come,
> And the glory of the LORD has risen upon you.
> For behold, darkness will cover the earth
> And deep darkness the peoples;
> But the LORD will rise upon you
> And His glory will appear upon you.

Father God, let Your glory rise upon Israel so that they shine brilliantly with Your presence. In the midst of much darkness in the Middle East and across the Earth, I ask that You rise upon Your people. Let Your glory appear upon Israel, and may the God of Israel be exalted. Reveal Your salvation like a burning torch to Your Jewish people worldwide. Pour out Your spirit of revelation and grant favor to the completed Jews among the Messianic movement and use them mightily among their people. For Your Kingdom's sake, amen.

Where Do We Go from Here?

By now you might be asking, "Are there any *more* surprises waiting in store for us, James Goll?" I think so! Let's stay like children in our hearts and be curious learners. Remember that Abraham laughed at the prospect of having a child with Sarah. Can you imagine his surprise and delight when, at an even older age, he fathered six additional sons through Keturah, his wife after the death of Sarah?

Let's look at the descendants of Keturah as we conclude this section on praying for the descendants of Abraham.

Reflection Questions

1. Who are the descendants of Sarah today?
2. What is the most important thing in the heart of God—the land of Israel or the hearts of the Israeli people? Why?
3. What are some of the scriptural prayers that you can bring before the hearing of the Lord on the Jewish people's behalf?

More Study Aids

Finto, Don. *Your People Shall Be My People*. Ventura, Calif.: Regal Books, 2001.

Hedding, Malcolm. *Understanding Israel*. Oklahoma City, Okla.: Zion's Gate International, 2002.

6 The Descendants of Keturah

> In that day Israel will be the third party with Egypt and Assyria, a blessing in the midst of the earth, whom the LORD of hosts has blessed, saying, "Blessed is Egypt My people, and Assyria the work of My hands, and Israel My inheritance."
>
> Isaiah 19:24–25

I want to speak in an honest and transparent manner as I begin this chapter. I have been reading the Bible for years and have thirty years of ministry under my belt at the time of this writing. But never once in my life have I ever heard a teaching on Keturah, let alone the prophetic destiny of her children.

I have been praying over this manuscript for the past three years. I thought I knew what I was going to compose. But along the way, the Holy Spirit kept divinely interrupting my path. Delay after delay occurred, and I often wondered what this "opposition" was all about. But as each "delay" transpired, God gave me additional understanding. I am not presenting myself as someone who knows it all but, like you, I am a work in progress. I know that I will, in fact, want to update this writing in five or fifteen years from now. With this perspective in mind, let's do some more pioneering by peering into the lives of *all* the descendants of Abraham.

Satisfied with Life

Abraham's wife Sarah lived almost forty years after the birth of Isaac. Genesis 23:1–2 says:

> Now Sarah lived one hundred and twenty-seven years; these were the years of the life of Sarah. Sarah died in Kiriath-arba (that is, Hebron) in the land of Canaan; and Abraham went in to mourn for Sarah and to weep for her.

Abraham loved Sarah dearly and must have experienced much grief and pain at her loss. After finding an excellent wife for his son Isaac, Abraham took another wife, whose name was Keturah. Genesis 25:2–4 says that Keturah

> bore to him Zimran and Jokshan and Medan and Midian and Ishback and Shuah. And Jokshan became the father of Sheba and Dedan. And the sons of Dedan were Asshurim and Letushim and Leummim. The sons of Midian were Ephah and Epher and Hanoch and Abida and Eldaah. All these were the sons of Keturah.

Keturah bore more children by Abraham than did Sarah and Hagar combined. I think that is interesting.

Before Abraham died he gave gifts to the sons of Keturah and sent them far away from his son Isaac, to the land of the east (see Genesis 25:6). One of the sons of Keturah was Midian, the father of the Midianites. Some of the descendants of

Keturah went to what was called Persia. Others were, apparently, scattered into Assyria.

Genesis 25:7–8 records:

> These are all the years of Abraham's life that he lived, one hundred and seventy-five years. Abraham breathed his last and died in a ripe old age, an old man and satisfied with life.

What a way to leave this Earth—as an old man satisfied with life, and with a lineage left behind!

Abraham's sons Isaac and Ishmael came together to bury their father in a cave. What a powerful statement! They came together—they united—to remember their father and put him to rest (see Genesis 25:9). I wonder if that could be a picture of things yet to come. Could it be that our Father will yet do such a work among the descendants of Abraham that they could come together in common purpose at some point and time in history?

Keturah's Descendants Will Praise the Lord

Isaiah prophesied about the descendants of Keturah, saying: "A multitude of camels will cover you [Israel], the young camels of Midian and Ephah" (Isaiah 60:6). Remember that Midian was a son of Keturah, and Ephah was her grandson. In the next part of this verse, Isaiah mentions yet another grandson of Keturah: Sheba. "All those from Sheba will come; they will bring gold and frankincense, and will bear good news of the praises of the Lord."

Where else have you heard of gold and frankincense together? They were two of the three gifts that the wise men brought to Jesus after His birth (see Matthew 2:1–12). I cannot confirm that the wise men were descendants of Keturah, but they did come from the east, where the descendants of Keturah had settled, and they certainly fit the description of Isaiah's prophecy.

Whether this prophecy was fulfilled literally at the birth of the Messiah or is a prophecy for the future yet to come, the minimum we can agree on is that there is prophetic destiny upon the children of Keturah. These people will rise up as people of wealth and will end up worshiping the one, true God. They will bring forth praise to the Lord!

Now let's go to the amazing prophecy of Isaiah, which has not yet been fulfilled. In this passage you will see the descendants of Hagar, Sarah and Keturah come together. As you read, keep in mind that Hagar was an Egyptian and that she returned to Egypt to find a wife for Ishmael, her half-Hebrew and half-Egyptian son. Remember, too, that the descendants of Keturah settled in Assyria and beyond.

> In that day there will be an altar to the Lord in the midst of the land of Egypt, and a pillar to the Lord near its border. It will become a sign and a witness to the Lord of hosts in the land of Egypt; for they will cry to the Lord because of oppressors, and He will send them a Savior and a Champion, and He will deliver them. . . .
>
> In that day there will be a highway from Egypt to Assyria, and the Assyrians will come into Egypt and the Egyptians into Assyria, and the Egyptians will worship with the Assyrians. In that day Israel will be the third party with Egypt and Assyria, a blessing in the midst of the earth, whom the Lord of hosts has blessed, saying, "Blessed is Egypt My people, and Assyria the work of My hands, and Israel My inheritance."
>
> Isaiah 19:20, 23–25

God is going to humble Egypt eventually, and Egypt is going to lift a cry for help. The Arabs are going to cry out due to the severity of their oppressors, and the Lord will manifest Himself as their Savior and Champion. After much pressure, and the probability of an all-out war in the Middle East, God will make Himself known to the Arabic peoples and they will turn to Him. Isaiah described the length to which they will go: "They will even worship with sacrifice and offering, and will make a vow to the Lord and perform it" (Isaiah 19:21). This not only means that they will have a God encounter, but that they will become true disciples and will walk in obedience.

Notice that this move of God will also impact Assyria: Turkey, Iraq, Iran and other Middle Eastern territories. Keturah's children were scattered throughout the vast lands of Assyria! They still have an identity today, but it is obscured because Abraham sent them all eastward into Trans Jordan and beyond (see Genesis 25:6).

Imagine—the very area of Asia Minor, where the early Church of Jesus Christ once flourished, will rise again out of the ashes into genuine, vibrant worship. Lands that appear to be held captive to the devil through Islam will be delivered and cleansed of their impurity. After thousands of years of broken promises, hatred and enmity between Arabs and Jews, this will truly be a glorious day! A day in history when the curse is reversed and the blessing of the Lord emerges. What a day that will be!

I can only imagine!

The Middle East is indeed a complex knot, but the Holy Spirit loves brooding over a mess of darkness. He is an expert at this task. Remember that the first mention of the Holy Spirit is that He hovered over the face of the deep. God loves bringing order out of chaos. The Holy Spirit is a pro at creating change and making all things new!

There will be, according to Isaiah, a highway from Egypt to Assyria, and people will go freely back and forth—probably right through the middle of Israel—worshiping God together. I can only imagine!

All of Abraham's Seed Will Be Blessed

The end of Isaiah 19 is so powerful that I want you to read it again:

> Israel will be the third party with Egypt and Assyria, a blessing in the midst of the earth, whom the Lord of hosts has blessed, saying,

> "Blessed is Egypt My people, and Assyria the work of My hands, and Israel My inheritance."
>
> Isaiah 19:24–25

Blessed are the descendants of Hagar, God's people! Blessed are the descendants of Keturah, the work of God's hands! Blessed are the descendants of Sarah, God's inheritance!

God is the supreme multitasker. He can accomplish more than one thing at a time! Biblical prophecy indicates that alongside God's gathering of the outcasts of Israel to their homeland, He is setting the stage to do a great work among all the descendants of Abraham. Surprise us all, O Lord. Let it be so!

Praying for All the Peoples of the Middle East

Isn't this good? God has declared a prophetic blessing over all the peoples of the Middle East, because they all have come from Abraham's seed. The devil has arisen, however, to thwart God's blessing. A holy war—an unholy war, rather—has raged for thousands of years. The conflict continues to intensify and a massive, satanic battle is coming. But I am here to declare that the Lord is going to pierce the veil of Islam. A move of God is going to come from out of Persia, out of Iraq, out of Syria, out of Lebanon, out of Egypt and, of course, out of Israel.

Times of Darkness Precede Times of Great Light

Now just to set the record straight: From the angle that I presently read the Scriptures, I see a lot of intense bickering and warfare yet to occur before the fullness of Isaiah 19 comes to pass. I am not an ostrich, with my head buried in the sand! Isaiah 60:1–3 lays out a scriptural principle that says a time of great darkness will precede the unveiling of a great light. Gentiles will come to the brightness of its shining, and even kings will bow to the brilliance of this great light. But first comes gross darkness.

Consider with me now Psalm 83:3–8, 16–18:

> They make shrewd plans against Your people,
> And conspire together against Your treasured ones.
> They have said, "Come and let us wipe them out as a nation,
> That the name of Israel be remembered no more."
> For they have conspired together with one mind;
> Against You they make a covenant:
> The tents of Edom and the Ishmaelites,
> Moab and the Hagrites;
> Gebal and Ammon and Amalek,
> Philistia with the inhabitants of Tyre;
> Assyria also has joined with them;
> They have become a help to the children of Lot. . . .
> Fill their faces with dishonor,
> That they may seek Your name, O Lord.
> Let them be ashamed and dismayed forever,
> And let them be humiliated and perish,
> That they may know that You alone, whose name is the Lord,
> Are the Most High over all the earth.

Many Bible teachers agree that this text has not yet been fulfilled. This particular group has not yet been brought into an alignment with this degree of hatred. The passage does not say "the peoples of the land of the north," nor does it say "Germany." In fact, even Egypt seems to be missing from this list! Who and what is this alliance that conspires together?

Psalm 83 describes vividly a troubling alignment set against a wearied Jewish state. Let's turn to the pen of Sandra Teplinsky for more details:

> Verses 5–8 tell how every nation in the neighborhood (except Egypt) unites against Israel: Edom and the Ishmaelites (southern Jordan and Saudi Arabia); Moab (central Jordan) and the Hagrites (Syria

> and Arabia); Gebal (southern Jordan); Ammon (central Jordan) and Amalek (Sinai desert); Philistia (Gaza Strip area); Tyre (southern Lebanon) and Assyria (Syria/Iraq). Verse 4 sounds their bellicose battle cry: "Come . . . let us destroy them as a nation, that the name of Israel be remembered no more."[1]

In some ways this is nothing new. As I laid out earlier the enemy has, from the inception of Israel's rebirth, been standing close by with a knife to cut her throat! How did God's prophetic psalmist respond to this threat? How should we respond when we see these things taking place? The psalmist calls for God to glorify Himself—to make His great name and His name alone known over all the Earth. God's goal in times of testing is to glorify Himself.

> He will ultimately use the Arab/Palestinian-Israeli conflict to do it. He wants both blood-drenched peoples to know that He alone is most High—not Allah, not Judaism without Jesus, not global secular humanism, not anything.[2]

What if the eyes of the entire world were looking on at the moment of Israel's imminent destruction—the moment when God brings humiliation to the enemies of Israel for the purpose of releasing His grace upon them?

Light Will Overpower the Darkness

Darkness comes first, and then the light shines (see John 1:5). There has never been a contest between light and darkness. When you enter a house, you simply flip the switch and (if it is wired properly) the light always drives away the darkness. Darkness is a temporary state! I am here not to declare the revival of evil—there are plenty of top-selling authors who will do that for you. I am here to broaden our horizons and to help us peer into the redemptive purposes of God, even in the midst of the most stressful, difficult times of the ages. Light will overpower darkness; eventually, somehow—someday!

The Scriptures I have shared regarding God's promises to the descendants of Abraham are all for this purpose: to bring light and hope to the very dark situation in the Middle East. But if all we had was Joel's prophecy we would still be assured that, before this world comes to an end, God will pour out His Spirit on all people (see Joel 2:28–29).

Target Practice

Somehow we made it to our Target Practice and you are still with me! Whew! (I thought for a moment I might have lost you!) Now let's set our sights with more Scripture-based praying.

Scripture and Prayer from Isaiah 19:23–25

> In that day there will be a highway from Egypt to Assyria, and the Assyrians will come into Egypt and the Egyptians into Assyria, and the Egyptians will worship with the Assyrians.
>
> In that day Israel will be the third party with Egypt and Assyria, a blessing in the midst of the earth, whom the Lord of hosts has blessed, saying, "Blessed is Egypt My people, and Assyria the work of My hands, and Israel My inheritance."

Heavenly Father, thank You for the many promises that You have given to me and that You will fulfill each one. Thank You that You will also fulfill every promise You made to Abraham and his descendants. Hasten the day when all the descendants of Abraham through Hagar, Sarah and Keturah will worship You together in one accord. I agree with Your Word that says the descendants of Keturah are the work of Your hands and will be a blessing in the Earth. I ask specifically that You would bless the descendants of Keturah and lead them to Yourself. Reveal to them that Yeshua *is their Messiah. I ask that Jesus would receive the reward of His sufferings through these descendants of Abraham, for the glory of Your holy and righteous name. Amen.*

Scripture and Prayer from Isaiah 60:6

> The young camels of Midian and Ephah;
> All those from Sheba will come;
> They will bring gold and frankincense,
> And will bear good news of the praises of the Lord.

Father God, I ask that the "young camels" and all the descendants of Keturah would come to You and turn favorably toward Israel. Bless them. Multiply them. Prosper them. I ask that You would inspire them to use their wealth to bless Israel and the Kingdom of God. I ask that they would be known in the Middle East and in the Earth as bearers of the good news of praises to the Lord. Establish them as worshipers of the God of their father, Abraham, for Your great name's sake. Amen.

Scripture and Prayer from Matthew 9:36–38

> Seeing the people, He [Jesus] felt compassion for them, because they were distressed and dispirited like sheep without a shepherd. Then He said to His disciples, "The harvest is plentiful, but the workers are few. Therefore beseech the Lord of the harvest to send out workers into His harvest."

Father God, Your compassion burned in the heart of Your Son, Jesus. Turn the distress of Abraham's descendants into gladness and blessing. I ask that their souls would not be downcast, but that they would put their hope in the God of their father, Abraham. Transform their misguided ways and lead them in Your paths of righteousness. Cause them to hunger and thirst after righteousness. Send out workers into this harvest field to bring Your living waters to a dry and weary land. I ask that Your workers would reap a bountiful harvest for Your Kingdom's sake. Amen.

Scripture and Prayer from John 10:14–16

> I am the good shepherd, and I know My own and My own know Me, even as the Father knows Me and I know the Father; and I lay down My life for the sheep. I have other sheep, which are not of

this fold; I must bring them also, and they will hear My voice; and they will become one flock with one shepherd.

Jesus, Yeshua, *Messiah, You are a good shepherd and You know all Your sheep. You have laid Your life down for all the descendants of Abraham through Hagar, Sarah and Keturah. Bring the descendants of Hagar and Keturah into Your fold. Quicken their ears to hear Your voice. I ask that they would join with the descendants of Israel so that all of Abraham's descendants will become one flock with You as their great Shepherd. You are a mighty God and You will bring Your word to pass for Your name's sake. Amen!*

The Promised Son of Abraham

All three national families of Abraham have, by and large, failed to recognize the true Messiah, who is *Yeshua*, our Lord Jesus Christ. The Jews are still looking for their Messiah to appear, while the others do not even realize that they need one. Although most accept Mohammed and Jesus as prophets, they do not believe that a Messiah is necessary. Still the prophetic Scriptures predict that these descendants of Abraham will accept the true Messiah at a critical point in time.

I love the language of Isaiah 19:20: "He will send them a Savior and a Champion." A champion shall come. A messenger of the new covenant will be sent to turn away ungodliness from Jacob. *Yeshua*, Jesus, the true Messiah, said it succinctly: "I have other sheep, which are not of this fold; I must bring them also, and they will hear My voice; and they will become one flock with one shepherd" (John 10:16). A great spiritual revival is on God's agenda, and it will encompass all the descendants of Abraham throughout the Middle East, from the Nile River to the Euphrates.

An Amazing Confirmation

As providence would have it, I was recently helping to lead an all-night Worship Watch in my hometown. Our last session, from 3:30 to 5:00 A.M., was an Israel Prayer Watch. I began to explain to the group how I had struggled in the composition of the book you are now reading. I described how, in the process of writing, I was the one who had become the student, having my heart expanded to pray for all the descendants of the Middle East.

When I finished, two young, beautiful ladies proceeded to the platform. One was a believing Messianic Jew. The other anointed young lady was from Iran and had escaped through Iraq to make pilgrimage into the United States. She was Persian with Jewish blood but also a believer in Jesus! Here we had the descendants of Sarah and Keturah right before our eyes.

Many of us were weeping over them in gratitude and intercession when, the next thing we knew, another dark-complexioned believer in the Messiah joined the other two on the platform. All three embraced. The third young lady was from northern Africa! Now we had a complete picture before our eyes: Three women united in weeping intercession that God's purposes in the Middle East would come to pass. Yes, God has some surprises in store for all of us! May the descendants of Hagar, Sarah and Keturah all find the one true God and embrace one another for Jesus' sake!

My Closing Prayer for the Descendants of Abraham

Father, I thank You right now. Though we do not fully comprehend, and we do not know how Your Word will unfold, You have a plan in Your heart that is enormous, so vast. So we cry out for the descendants of Ishmael, that the blinders would fall off of their eyes for the sake of Yeshua's *holy name. You say that one day kings will come to the brightness of Your shining. We pray that the descendants of Keturah, who were sent eastward, will return bringing gold and frankincense to worship the one true God, and to give Him praise and glory.*

So we thank You, for whether that prophecy has been fulfilled or not, it shall be. We thank You! We call forth Keturah's prophetic destiny to come into being. We pray for the descendants of Sarah as well. We pray that the blinders would come off of the Jewish people's eyes. The book of Romans says that Israel will come when the times of the fullness of the Gentiles are fulfilled. We bless the descendants of Keturah and Hagar, who are Gentiles, and ask that the fullness of these Gentiles will come and that they in turn will help release the blinders from the Jewish people's eyes. Amen and amen!

Now on to our appointment in Jerusalem—a city of destiny![3]

Reflection Questions

1. Who are the descendants of Keturah today?
2. What are the prophetic promises of Scripture for the descendants of Keturah?
3. What blessings can you pray for the peoples of Iran, Iraq, Jordan, Syria and the other lands of the Middle East?

More Study Aids

Somerville, Robert. *The Three Families of Abraham*. Huntsville, Ala.: Awareness Ministry, 2002.

Archbold, Norma. *The Mountains of Israel*. Jerusalem, Israel: Phoebe's Song Publication, 1993.

Part 3

Praying for the Fullness of God's Purposes

7

Jerusalem: A City of Destiny

> I have chosen Jerusalem that My name might be there, and I have chosen David to be over My people Israel.
>
> 2 Chronicles 6:6

In ancient times maps displayed Jerusalem as the center of the Earth. It is the only city in the entire Bible that we are commanded to pray for by name. Jerusalem is mentioned 881 times in the Scriptures! Psalm 122:6–9 declares:

> Pray for the peace of Jerusalem:
> "May they prosper who love you.
> May peace be within your walls,
> And prosperity within your palaces."
> For the sake of my brothers and my friends,
> I will now say, "May peace be within you."
> For the sake of the house of the LORD our God,
> I will seek your good.

While God has given each of us the priestly privilege of interceding for our respective cities and nations, no city but Jerusalem is mentioned as one that every God-fearing believer must pray for. Jerusalem is a city where east meets west; a city of great contrasts, great conflicts and a great destiny. It is considered holy by Christians, Jews and Muslims alike. It is indeed a unique city, both in the world and in the heart of God.

According to the Central Bureau of Statistics, Jerusalem is home to 692,300 residents, and is both the country's most populous city and its largest geographically (twice as big as Tel Aviv). The city's population grew in 2003 by some 12,000 residents, reflecting a growth rate of 1.7 percent.

In 2002, 66 percent of the residents were Jewish, 31 percent Muslim and 2 percent Christian. Children under the age of fifteen made up 35 percent of the city's population. Some 53 percent attended ultra-Orthodox schools and 28 percent went to secular schools. Jerusalem Center for Israel Research figures show that secular Israelis have been steadily moving out of the capital.[1] Is there a trend here? Is Jerusalem becoming more and more a "religious conservative center"?

In my travels around the world, I have found that Jerusalem is truly a city like no other. It gets under your skin! It slips into your heart. I remember when Michal Ann and I were leading a prayer tour of Israel with Avner Boskey of Final Frontier Ministries and, while traveling on our bus, we listened to the marvelous music of cantor Marty Goetz. While the setting sun cast golden highlights on the white stones of the city of Jerusalem, we sang the words of Isaiah and wept together: "For Zion's sake I will not keep silent. For Jerusalem's sake I will not keep quiet." How our hearts burned with God's desires for His beloved city! Jerusalem is indeed a city where the past, the present and the future meet.

The psalmist described it this way:

> How can we sing the songs of the Lord
> while in a foreign land?
> If I forget you, O Jerusalem,

may my right hand forget its skill.
May my tongue cling to the roof of my mouth
if I do not remember you,
if I do not consider Jerusalem
my highest joy.

Psalm 137:4–6, NIV

Do you also carry Jerusalem in your heart?

Next Year in Jerusalem!

For centuries the Jewish people have wandered, exiled from their homeland and exiled from their beloved Jerusalem, the city of David—the city of God! Rejected by nation after nation, the Jewish people were forced to become pilgrims, without a place to rest their heads.

If you listen closely enough you can hear the weeping of Israel's children down through the centuries, as they dreamed of returning to the Promised Land. A river of tears flows through the pages of time as God's people prayed for deliverance and cried out, "Next year in Jerusalem!"

The First Crusade successfully captured Jerusalem in the summer of 1099, but the crusaders spent their first week in the Holy City slaughtering the Jews and Muslims there. One historian says the men "heartily devoted the day to exterminating Jewish men, women, and children—killing more than 10,000."[2] Ownership of this Middle Eastern city has been contested more than that of any other city in the world. But yet the cry still arises, "Next year in Jerusalem!"

Jews in Muslim countries have been hanged in the public squares. Jews were marked for destruction in the gas chambers in Treblinka and in the ovens of Auschwitz. Still a desperate cry rang out from the heart of a wandering people. From the frozen tundra of Siberia to the hot sands of the Ethiopian desert, they cried out: "Next year in Jerusalem!"

History Speaks

History speaks and we must listen to her wisdom. Often, to our chagrin, history speaks with a deafening silence. It could be argued that the United States has been Israel's greatest ally in recent history, but other pages of American history are not as glorious. Franklin D. Roosevelt was the last American President during World War II who could have taken direct action to prevent the deaths of six million Jews during the Holocaust. In the middle of the greatest war ever fought, with over three million Jewish people already executed, Roosevelt was still eerily silent on the matter. It appears that the man considered America's greatest Democratic president was also part of our darkest hour as a nation. In that bleak hour, America and the nations of the world closed their ears to the piercing cries of the Jewish people.

In December 1939, Roosevelt appointed Breckenridge Long to the prominent position of determining who would and would not receive entry permits from Nazi Germany into the United States. Long's philosophy was simple and troubling: "Keep them all out; they are all troublemakers." When once questioned about what should happen to the Jews trying to escape Hitler, Long replied by using his hands as an imaginary machine gun to mow them all down.[3]

I remember visiting the Dachau concentration camp with Michal Ann, back in the 1970s. My father's family is primarily of German descent, and I was stunned by the lingering evidence of what my people had done. How could such atrocities occur in modern civilization? It was as though I could still hear the cries of the Jewish people echoing in those vacant barracks.

Evidence suggests that President Roosevelt and the State Department already knew something definite about Hitler's "Final Solution to the Jewish Problem" in 1942.[4] With the United States already engaged in the war, it seemed probable that the U.S. would either help to find a safe haven for the Jewish people or else at least use the verifiable information about German atrocities as a rallying cry for the war. Neither happened! But in spite of this, the defiant cry still rang out from inside the Nazi death camps—"Next year in Jerusalem!"

According to the U.S. State Department, it has been foreign policy since 1948 not to recognize any part of Jerusalem as "Israel" unless the entire Arab world does so first. This includes the section of west Jerusalem that has been a part of Israel since 1948, and which will remain under Israeli control under any Arab-Israeli agreement.

The late George C. Marshall, the secretary of state under Harry S. Truman, heavily influenced the U.S. State Department policy regarding Israel.[5] It is well documented that Marshall was strongly, even rabidly, against Truman recognizing the Jewish state. During a policy meeting regarding the recognition of Israel, Marshall went so far as to tell the president: "If you follow Clifford's [Truman's secretary of defense] advice, and if I were to vote in the election, I would vote against you." Those were quite strong words from a secretary of state to a sitting president!

Clifford said in his memoirs, "Officials in the State Department had done everything in their power to prevent, thwart, or delay the President's Palestine policy in 1947 and 1948."[6]

The bias in the State Department continues to this day, as a recently-released human rights report portrays. Only a short portion of the document is dedicated to the attacks against Israel by terror groups. The balance of the document details Israel's "failures" in the area of human rights. No mention is made that many of the supposed infringements on human rights are essential to protecting Israeli citizens from an onslaught of suicide bombers.

An American couple whose son was born in Israel has filed suit because the U.S. State Department will not allow the parents to register their baby's place of birth as "Jerusalem, Israel." The places of birth in all other instances are determined by the applicant's wishes and, of course, the place of actual birth. Only in Jerusalem does the U.S. State Department refuse to accede to the applicants' wishes. Something does not add up here!

Now for some good news! The 104th Congress of the United States of America passed Public Law 104/45, the Jerusalem Embassy Act, in 1995. This document officially recognizes Jerusalem as the capital of Israel. Amazing! Wonderful! Awesome! And that is not all—Public Law 104/45 also allocates $25 million to move the U.S. Embassy to Jerusalem.

While that is great news, the enactment of this law continues to be held up in political quagmire. Why does the U.S. government not move forward in recognizing Jerusalem as Israel's capital when it has, in fact, been the capital of Israel for 3,300 years—since the days of King David? Why have presidential waivers continued to postpone this act every six months since it passed in Congress? Can we not take a stand? Is our word not our bond? It is time for our actions to speak louder than our words!

The reasons behind this waffling governmental position are complex indeed. Or perhaps they boil down to plain old self-interest and self-protection. There are those who persist in saying that moving our embassy to Jerusalem would create a national security threat to the U.S. The real reason is plain and simple: Arabic countries do not want the U.S. to recognize Jerusalem as Israel's capital, and we bow to their pressure. If we did not bow, why, it might create such a stir that the international community might have to recognize Israel's right to exist!

It is time for new Winston Churchills and Harry S. Trumans to arise. I am not endorsing all their decisions, nor declaring that all their actions were righteous. But when they spoke—the buck stopped there! The shouts of "Never give up!" must be heard again. Let's pray for our governmental leaders to take a stand for ethical justice, for the State of Israel and for the city of Jerusalem. You see, each time the national security waiver is signed, we are saying to terrorists and enemies of Israel, "You win."

America needs the blessings of God more than favor with sheikhs and Arab oil. No longer should America and the nations allow terrorists to threaten us into choosing political expediency over moral clarity. If we as a nation can wage a worldwide war on terror, why do we refuse to allow Israel to do the same within her own borders and region?

Former New York City Mayor Rudolph Giuliani had the courage to say, "No, thank you," to a gift from an Arab sheikh who had linked 9/11 to our political support of Israel. Our other government officials need to have a similar moral fortitude. America and the nations of the world are in a state of moral decay. It is time for our leaders to let the godfather of world terrorism, the architect of the Munich massacre and the financiers of murderous suicide bombings know that the party is over. It is time to allow the Jerusalem Embassy Act to become law and move the U.S. Embassy to Jerusalem!

Jerusalem: Her Many Names

The meaning of a name given to a person, family, city or nation often reveals a portion of its prophetic destiny. Glimpses into divine purpose peek through the veil when we correctly interpret and gain understanding of our names.

Cities and regions often live to have more than one name, particularly if they come under the rule of different regimes and cultures. Consider the beautiful city of Saint Petersburg, Russia. This northern port city was not long ago called Leningrad of the Soviet Union. The original name, Saint Petersburg, takes an obvious influence from church history. But when communism ruled, it was given a new title that represented a contrasting spirit of atheism. Times change, leaders rise and fall and the names of places often change with each season, leaving behind a special part of history or piece of destiny yet to be fulfilled. So it is with Jerusalem.

The inspired authors of Scripture have given this unique city many names over the centuries. Consider with me some of her names as recorded throughout biblical history, and we will peek together into her prophetic destiny.[7]

- City of David—2 Samuel 6:10; 1 Kings 11:27; 2 Chronicles 8:11
- City of God—Psalm 46:4; Psalm 87:3
- City of Judah—2 Chronicles 25:28
- City of Joy—Jeremiah 49:25
- City of Peace—Hebrews 7:2
- City of Praise—Jeremiah 49:25
- City of Righteousness—Isaiah 1:26
- City of the Great King—Psalm 48:2; Matthew 5:35
- City of the Lord—Isaiah 60:14
- City of Truth—Zechariah 8:3
- Faithful City—Isaiah 1:26
- Gate of My People—Obadiah 1:13; Micah 1:9
- Green Olive Tree—Jeremiah 11:16
- Holy City—Nehemiah 11:1, 18; Isaiah 48:2; 52:1; Matthew 4:5; 27:53; Revelation 11:2
- Holy Mountain—Isaiah 11:9; 56:7; 57:13; 65:25; 66:20; Ezekiel 20:40; Daniel 9:16, 20; Joel 2:1; 3:17; Zephaniah 3:11; Zechariah 8:3
- Throne of the Lord—Jeremiah 3:17
- Zion—1 Kings 8:1; Isaiah 60:14; Zechariah 9:13

Wow! Jerusalem is called everything from the City of God to the Holy City. It looks to me like there must still be a lot of His Story (history) yet to come to pass in the destiny of Jerusalem.

For a great description of this unique city, let's gaze into the psalms:

Beautiful in elevation, the joy of the whole earth,
Is Mount Zion in the far north,
The city of the great King. . . .
Walk about Zion and go around her;
Count her towers;
Consider her ramparts;
Go through her palaces,
That you may tell it to the next generation.

Psalm 48:2, 12–13

Surely Your servants find pleasure in her stones
And feel pity for her dust.

Psalm 102:14

Jerusalem, that is built
As a city that is compact together.

Psalm 122:3

As the mountains surround Jerusalem,
So the Lord surrounds His people
From this time forth and forever.

Psalm 125:2

Yes, it is true; Jerusalem is a dusty city surrounded by worn mountains. She is a congested, compacted city full of large and small stones. These stones have been used to build architectural wonders, and they have been hurled as tools of destruction. But there is none like her.

Songs are written about you, Jerusalem. Writers are fond of your winding streets and the diverse personalities of your people. Prophets declare your future. Intercessors weep, as Jesus did, that you would yet come under the wings of your Messiah.

Jerusalem is a place of destiny! God has already set countless divine appointments within this city, the heart of Israel. It was King David's capital, the home to Levites and priests and the place where Israel's holy feasts were observed. The Temple was built in Jerusalem, and the Holy Spirit was first poured out in Jerusalem—the place God's people have always loved. Jerusalem is a place like no other, a city where future appointments on God's calendar are yet to be fulfilled.[8]

A Heavy Stone to Carry

Jerusalem is a prophetic city of great contrasts. The prophet Zechariah warned sternly:

> Behold, I am going to make Jerusalem a cup that causes reeling to all the peoples around; and when the siege is against Jerusalem, it will also be against Judah. It will come about in that day that I will make Jerusalem a heavy stone for all peoples; all who lift it will be severely injured. And all the nations of the earth will be gathered against it.
>
> Zechariah 12:2–3

Nations and entire empires have risen and fallen depending on how they have treated this unusual city and its inhabitants. It somehow either releases a blessing or exudes a curse, and we can choose between the two. Ultimately a day will come, the great and terrible day of the Lord, when all nations of the Earth will be caught in a divine vortex as they are gathered against Jerusalem.

In the midst of this, my prayer and expectant hope is that a body of believers will arise and be Israel's best friend in that hour. The shout, "Israel, you are not alone," will be heard from interceding friends whose hearts have been broken with the things that break God's heart. Though Jerusalem is a "heavy stone to carry," God gives grace to carry the burden. He must! It is His Kingdom way!

As for me and my house, I see no other choice than to care for Jerusalem and the destiny of her inhabitants. I want more than anything to be close to the heart of God. I choose with honor, therefore, to pick up this stone and carry it with the love of Christ.

Pray for the Shalom of Jerusalem

If there is any area where we desperately need to have revelation, it is in the area of praying "for the peace of Jerusalem." In these confusing days of multiple peace plans—the Oslo Accord, the Quartet Road Map and who knows what comes next—there is overwhelming evidence that we do not really know what it means to "pray for the peace" of Jerusalem! Yet we have a mandate from heaven to intercede!

Let's consider the word "peace."

The Hebrew word for peace is *shalom*, and this word has a much deeper meaning than the mere absence of conflict or war. A cease-fire is never peace, not even if it becomes permanent. A "cold war" was never God's idea.[9] This form of peace is a purely human contrivance for keeping warring parties separated so that they do not get the opportunity to destroy one another. Such a peace is unknown to God!

Shalom has, in the Hebrew, several different facets to its meaning, but they all have the same intent. It can mean "to be completed" in regard to God's purposes and plans. It can also mean "to be restored," meaning to enter into the fullness of one's calling. When we pray for the peace of Jerusalem, we are actually asking the Lord to bring Jerusalem into her divine destiny and to let her be restored into the fullness of God's calling.[10]

No one in his or her right mind could ever think that "peace" will be achieved in the Middle East without a season of conflict, suffering and even war. If a sane person does believe that, he or she is simply not a student of either God's Word or history! The current international peace process has little of God's interests in mind. There will never be true, lasting peace without the Prince of Peace being in the middle of the process!

Shalom can also mean "healing," because the Hebrew words for "restore" and "heal" come from the same root. In the meaning of "healing," we can see something very interesting about the present peace process.[11] Listen to God's view on this matter: "They heal the brokenness of the daughter of My people superficially, saying, 'Peace, peace,' but there is no peace" (Jeremiah 8:11).

This says to me that at the very end of the age, before the glorious coming of the Messiah, the international focus will be on "peace." Even the United Nations takes a verse of Scripture out of context and has it inscribed on the outside of its great facade! "They shall beat their swords into plowshares, and their spears into pruning hooks; nation shall not lift up sword against nation, neither shall they learn war any more" (Micah 4:3, RSV). The UN and other secular, humanist world organizations think that they can bring about a true and lasting peace by their own efforts. What a delusion!

So what are we to do? There is no such thing as true and lasting peace without a relationship with God. Peace is not just a feeling. Peace is not just a condition. True peace is a Person—the Son of God, the Messiah, King of the Jews! There is no peace for any person, family, neighborhood, city or nation without the Prince of Peace! So when I pray for the "peace of Jerusalem," I am ultimately interceding that the blinders will fall off the eyes of all unbelievers and that they will behold and embrace the beautiful Messiah Jesus!

Peace has been made for us through the blood of the cross (see Colossians 1:20). You cannot bypass the cross of *Yeshua* on the path to peace! Yes, let's do all we can to bring an end to conflict, war and terror. Let's sit at the negotiation tables and work for reconciliation. But to pray for the *shalom* of Jerusalem is to pray that the Jewish people will be reconciled to the God of Israel. The same is true for all the descendants of Abraham—Arab, Jew and all Gentile peoples alike! The *shalom* of Jerusalem means that she will be completed in God's purposes and reach her divine destiny in the Messiah. That, and that alone, is true *shalom*.

Target Practice

Now it is time to get ready and fire our bullets of Scripture-based prayer in defense of Jerusalem, her unique destiny and her role in the Earth.

Scripture and Prayer from 2 Chronicles 7:15–16

Now My eyes will be open and My ears attentive to the prayer offered in this place. For now I have chosen and consecrated this house that My name may be there forever, and My eyes and My heart will be there perpetually.

Father, in the Messiah's great name, we ask that You lean Your ear once again toward Jerusalem, the city You have chosen. Be attentive to the prayers uttered by Your chosen people. Lean Your ear and hear the decades of cries at the Wailing Wall. You say that Your eyes and Your heart will always be there. Look now and hear the groans of Your covenant people. Answer quickly in Your great mercy and may Your name be established there forever! O Lord, act for Your holy name's sake! Amen!

Scripture and Prayer from Psalm 122:6–7

Pray for the peace of Jerusalem:
"May they prosper who love you.
May peace be within your walls,
And prosperity within your palaces."

Father God, send Your shalom *to Jerusalem. Let Your Kingdom come! Let the Prince of Peace—the Messiah Himself—be revealed and let His will be done. May the blinders come off both Jew and*

Gentile eyes alike! Prosper those who love You. Bring Your shalom *within the walls of Jerusalem. Prosper the spiritual leadership of Israel, our president and the leaders of all nations. Impart Your heart to all those in governmental authority. Release Your peace and the revelation that the ultimate Source of eternal peace and salvation is the Messiah,* Yeshua. *Establish Jerusalem as a praise in the Earth for Your glory's sake! Amen!*

Scripture and Prayer from Acts 1:4

> Gathering them together, He commanded them not to leave Jerusalem, but to wait for what the Father had promised, "Which," He said, "you have heard of from Me."

Father God, send an unprecedented outpouring of Your glorious presence upon the city of Jerusalem once again like You did two thousand years ago. Send a new Pentecost upon the believers in the land. Send the promise of the Father upon the inhabitants of Jerusalem. Let the fire of Your Spirit fall! Let the wind blow the sound of it forth to gather a crowd! Send forth the promise of the Father upon the city of Jerusalem for Your holy name's sake! Amen!

A Special Day Each Year

I doubt that there has ever been a more crucial time for believers to gather in prayer for Jerusalem. The battle for Israel and Jerusalem is, ultimately, the battle for Judeo-Christian presence in the world and the future of Western civilization as we know it. American Christians have too often been vague and unempowered in their connection with this world-shaping problem. But the understanding that we must become informed intercessors and empower those in our circle of influence to lift their voices to the Lord is growing in the evangelical Christian community.

An International Day of Prayer for the Peace of Jerusalem (IDPPJ) has, therefore, been declared for the first Sunday of every October (a date near Yom Kippur). This is a call for the global Church to set aside one day each year to fulfill the biblical mandate in Psalm 122:6 and other Scriptures, to pray for the peace of Jerusalem and for all of her inhabitants. The resolution calling for this prayer observance has been signed by hundreds of Christian leaders of influence from around the world, representing tens of millions of believers.

The IDPPJ is endorsed by a broad coalition of Christian leadership from many nations and church backgrounds. Each of these leaders has joined in signing the call to prayer, calling the Church around the world to pray for the peace of all the inhabitants of Jerusalem. The initiative is cochaired by Rev. Robert Stearns, executive director of Eagles' Wings Ministries, and Dr. Jack Hayford, president and founder of the Kings College and Seminary.

My wife and I are among the many endorsers of this strategic prayer initiative. Churches, ministries and individual believers across the globe are encouraged to participate and can learn more from the Day to Pray website. The following is the adopted Resolution to Pray agreed upon by the IDPPJ:

RESOLUTION for a CALL to PRAYER

UNDERSTANDING—that we are children of Abraham by faith, the "wild olive branch" grafted in to the root of God's covenant, and

RECOGNIZING—that God has kept his word to Abraham and His descendants and settled them in their homeland again, according to the word of the prophets, and

RECOGNIZING—that we have a biblical mandate according to Psalm 122, and many other Scriptures to seek the good and prosperity of Jerusalem, until the Lord makes her a praise in all the Earth, and

AFFIRMING—that God's love and intended blessing is for all nations and peoples, and that we have goodwill and love for all mankind, including all inhabitants of the Holy Land, and desire the peace of this entire region;

> WE, the undersigned, call upon all men and women of prayer to yearly set aside the First Sunday in October, near the season of Yom Kippur, as the DAY of PRAYER for the PEACE of JERUSALEM.[12]

Join us and the growing prayer army across the world in this crucial hour of history, and pray for the peace of Jerusalem, a city of destiny.

Reflection Questions

1. What are some of the biblical names given to Jerusalem?
2. Jerusalem is called both a "heavy stone" and a "glorious diadem" for the Lord. What does this mean to you?
3. What does it mean to pray for the peace of Jerusalem?

More Study Aids

Derek Prince. *Promised Land, God's Word and the Nation of Israel*. Charlotte, N.C.: Derek Prince Ministries, 2003.

Evans, Michael D. *The American Prophecies*. New York: Time Warner Books, 2004.

8
Praying for the Fulfillment of *Aliyah*

> Do not fear, for I am with you;
> I will bring your offspring from the east,
> And gather you from the west.
> I will say to the north, "Give them up!"
> And to the south, "Do not hold them back."
> Bring My sons from afar
> And My daughters from the ends of the earth.
>
> Isaiah 43:5–6

The word *aliyah* might be foreign to your ear or biblical understanding. But the term is used commonly in the Semitic languages, especially Hebrew. *Aliyah,* simply put, means "to go up, to ascend; to go from a lower to a higher place." Over time *aliyah* has become associated with the journey of Hebrew families up to Jerusalem and the Temple

Mount, there to celebrate the three great annual festivals that the Lord ordained. Psalms were written to accompany these joyous occasions; fathers led their families up the highway to Jerusalem singing the psalms of *aliyah*.[1]

Over the years, the word *aliyah* has become very dear to both Jewish people and believing Gentiles alike. As prophetic Scriptures about the regathering of the Jewish people from the ends of the Earth are fulfilled right before our eyes, the term has become a way of describing all that is involved in the process of returning to the homeland.

The Forming and Preserving of a Nation

How could a remnant of scattered and persecuted Jewish people, who went through their darkest hour in Hitler's Holocaust, come forth all at once as a sovereign nation within their age-old boundaries? Surely it was with divine intervention, although many secular Israelis today believe they did it all on their own! Let's take a peek at some of the history behind the scenes.

Following World War I, in 1920, the League of Nations turned the control of "Palestine" over to Britain. Fear of Arab reprisals gradually turned British hearts against the Jewish immigrants who had been trickling back into the land since the turn of the century. Fear turned into politics, as the allowable quota of returning Jews was lowered and Israeli refugees were forbidden to land in Haifa Harbor.

As World War II commenced, the British government seemed to forget entirely its earlier commitment to protect *all* the citizens of Palestine. Jewish immigrants who arrived in Palestine, fleeing the Nazi persecution, were sent back to their cities of origin or—even worse—held in detention camps in nearby Cyprus. Other governments joined Britain in her indifference as gross atrocities were committed both in Nazi Germany and in Palestine. The establishment of a

Jewish nation now rested in the shaky hands of the United Nations.

On November 29, 1947, the General Assembly of the United Nations adopted a resolution requiring the establishment of a Jewish state in Palestine, and Jewish people around the world danced for joy. But within three days more than 40 million Arabs pitted themselves against the 600,000 Jews already living in Israel. Declaring a holy war, or *jihad*, Arab leaders vowed publicly, "We are going to kill all the Jews or drive them into the sea."

The enemies of Israel were so cocky that they warned all the Arabic people who were then living peacefully within the borders of the Jewish partition to move out of their homes so that they would not be caught up in the Israelis' destruction. This is, ironically, the true origin of the Palestinian refugees!

Few people today realize that four dreadful months of a battle for survival transpired in Palestine before the UN took its resolution to a full vote before the entire General Assembly. Finally, on May 14, 1948 (it was actually one minute past midnight on May 15), David Ben-Gurion read the following Proclamation of Independence:

> The land of Israel was the birthplace of the Jewish people. Here their spiritual, religious and national identity was formed. Here they achieved independence and created a culture of national and universal significance. Here they wrote and gave the Bible to the world. Exiled from the land of Israel, the Jewish people remained faithful to it in all the countries of their dispersion, never ceasing to pray and hope for their return and the restoration of their national freedom.
>
> Our call goes out to the Jewish people all over the world to rally to our side in the task of immigration and development and to stand by us in the great struggle for the fulfillment of the dream of generations for the redemption of Israel.
>
> With trust in Almighty God, we set our hand to this Declaration on the Sabbath eve, the fifth of Iyar, 5708, the fourteenth day of May, 1948.[2]

Not one full day later, five Arab nations assaulted the newborn Jewish nation. Egypt, Syria, Jordan, Lebanon and Iraq (forty million Arabs, with 1.5 million of them armed) attacked Israel in what became known as the Israeli War of Independence. This violent conflict continued for eight long months with heavy casualties on all sides. It was indeed a miracle that Israel, which had just been reborn, was not totally destroyed (see Isaiah 54:17). A tiny strip of land in the middle of the Earth was set apart once again for the Jewish people. A nation was born. Exiles returned, and the desert began to blossom. But peace did not last long.

In 1967 came the infamous Six-Day War. Once again it was a war that should have ended in disaster for Israel, but God's great mercy prevailed. At the end of six days, the Israelis occupied Sinai, the Gaza Strip, the West Bank and the Golan Heights. This conflict resulted in the amazing capture of the Old Jewish Quarter of Jerusalem and the remaining portion of the Western (Wailing) Wall of the Temple. Then came a season of peace, like a brief breath between birth pangs, and the Yom Kippur assault.

Consider with me the outcome of the 1973 surprise Yom Kippur assault: The Arabs, backed by the Soviet Union, attacked Israel on two fronts simultaneously. Taken off guard on their highest holy day, the Israelis were pushed back as the Arabs made quick territorial gains. Yet, by what I and many other intercessors believe was divine intervention, Israel regained all her land. Again the hand of God, working through the agency of human beings, released divine protection to the outnumbered and despised Jewish nation.

Prophetic Foreshadows

This history of God's providential protection of Israel since its rebirth as a nation in 1948 is a brilliant study in its own right. The amazing promise of God's restoration and protection of Israel is not based on anything good she has ever accomplished as a nation. It is rather a declaration of God's nature—His greatness and faithfulness. God and God alone will be glorified as this act of redemption unfolds. This is what mercy is all about! If Israel deserved pardon, she would not need God's grace. It is only through receiving His grace that she can restore to Him the glory of which her sins have robbed Him. Paul, the Jewish apostle to the Gentiles, paints this picture for us brilliantly in Romans 11:6: "If it is by grace, it is no longer on the basis of works, otherwise grace is no longer grace."

Let's take another glance at some of the remarkable Old Testament prophecies regarding Israel's dispersion and regathering.

Jeremiah's Detailed Declaration

Jeremiah, the weeping prophet spoken of earlier, gazed through the lens of time to reveal that Israel's covenant-keeping God would graciously offer His stretched-out wings as a place of divine protection specifically during the time of their gathering to the Promised Land:

> Hear the word of the Lord, O nations,
> And declare in the coastlands afar off,
> And say, "He who scattered Israel will gather him
> And keep him as a shepherd keeps his flock."
>
> Jeremiah 31:10

Jeremiah declared God's precise will to the Gentile nations. This was a prophetic declaration that God would perform a sovereign extraction of the Jewish peoples and that *aliyah* would be fulfilled. Amazing!

In this one short verse we find three great truths: First, it was God Himself who scattered Israel from her homeland. Second, the same God who scattered Israel will gather her back to her own land. Third, God will not merely gather Israel, but will keep her and put a divine hedge of protection around her as she is being gathered. What a promise! What a God!

Hosea's Piercing Pronouncement

The parabolic prophet Hosea adds another layer of truth. Listen to his penetrating words: [It will come about that] "in the place where it is said to them, 'You are not My people,' it will be said to them, 'You are the sons of the living God'" (Hosea 1:10).

This piercing prophetic statement, "You are not My people," was pronounced at a time when Israel languished in a state of rebellion and sin (see Hosea 1:9). But thank the Lord, God's word of judgment also included a ray of hope! Isn't it amazing? With every word of judgment there also comes a silver lining, a promise waiting to be found. God's true word cuts deeply at times, but these cuts are for the purpose of bringing healing and restoration.

On the heels of His judgment, God offered the Hebrew children a phenomenal promise. The land of Israel was the place where they were told they were not His people. He promised that in that place, in the land of Israel, "It will be said to them, 'You are the sons of the living God.'"

Contemplate the meaning of this verse more closely with me now: Hosea 1:10 speaks not only of a physical relocation and restoration, but also of a spiritual rebirth or revival that will take place among God's covenant people when they have returned to their covenant-given land. God is declaring a miracle of major proportions indeed. This is one of the major reasons *aliyah* is so important! No wonder the return of the Jewish people is so hotly contested in the spirit world! I agree with Malcolm Hedding, former chaplain of the International Christian Embassy Jerusalem, when he states:

> Israel's restoration is truly an eschatological event. That is, an event that has to do with the end of one age and with the beginning of another. The world is now in the *terminal season.*[3]

Whether or not you fully accept that premise, you must agree with me that the fulfillment of *aliyah* is a reflection of the awesome faithfulness of our Father! I once heard the late international Bible teacher Derek Prince declare, "To pass off the restoration of Israel as a political accident is like believing the world is flat!" Even after hundreds of years, God is faithful and true to His word!

Two Regatherings Were Prophesied

With the foundation of God's grace and faithfulness in place, let's add a few more building blocks to our understanding. With this next layer I want to expand our appreciation of the Diaspora (the dispersion) of the Jewish people throughout history. William W. Orr stated in 1948: "There isn't the slightest doubt that the emergence of the nation Israel among the family of nations is the greatest piece of prophetic news that we have had in the twentieth century." Such a significant event requires closer investigation if we are to truly grasp its significance, especially in view of the fact that a nation twice exiled has returned to the very land of its fathers. Such a thing is without precedent in world history.[4]

The First Regathering

Scripture foretold plainly that the Jewish people would suffer two major dispersions, or scatterings, from their own land, followed by two miraculous regatherings.

The first scattering was in the years when the prophets Daniel and Ezekiel were exiled in the land of Babylon, that period in which the Jews of the Judean kingdom were displaced from their country after the destruction of the Temple and of Jerusalem itself by Nebuchadnezzar (see Daniel 1:1–6). It was around 605 BC when Daniel and his associates were carried away. Their restoration to the land began in 538 BC (see 2 Chronicles 36:22–23; Ezra 1:1–4), and the Temple remained in ruins until 515 BC (see Ezra 6:15), about seventy years after its destruction in 587 BC.

In chapter 3, we considered the prayer life of Daniel. Let's take a moment now to review and expand on that understanding.

Daniel, a prophet of the one true God and a man of excellent character, was in captivity with the children of Israel in Babylon. It was perhaps their 63rd year of captivity in a foreign land with a foreign culture, foreign gods and foreign ways. Daniel was meditating on the Word of God (see Daniel 9:2) when a revelation based on the promises of Jeremiah came to him:

> "This whole land will be a desolation and a horror, and these nations will serve the king of Babylon seventy years.
>
> Then it will be when seventy years are completed I will punish the king of Babylon and that nation," declares the Lord.
>
> Jeremiah 25:11–12

> Thus says the Lord, "When seventy years have been completed for Babylon, I will visit you and fulfill My good word to you, to bring you back to this place."
>
> Jeremiah 29:10

Daniel believed the Word, and he declared it as true for his time and people—that at the end of seventy years of Babylonian captivity, the children of Israel would be released from their enslavement and return to their own land. Daniel sought the Lord for any reasons or blockades that might yet stand in the way of the promise of the Lord being fulfilled (see Daniel 9:3–19). Then, as described in my book on prophetic intercession, *Kneeling on the Promises*, Daniel responded to the word of revelation by humbly and persistently "kneeling on it."[5] He entered with resolution into *identificational repentance* and confessed the sins of his people as his own. The following verse summarizes his confession: "O Lord, hear! O Lord, forgive! O Lord, listen and take action! For Your own sake, O my God, do not delay, because Your city and Your people are called by Your name" (Daniel 9:19).

At the end of seventy years the Israelites were released into the fulfillment of prophecy—their first return to their covenant land. The walls of Jerusalem began to be rebuilt. The people returned. Restoration occurred!

The fact that the word of the Lord happened precisely as had been declared through the lips of Jeremiah and knelt upon by the prophet Daniel gives us an example of prophetic intercession at its best. Many more cycles of faith, sin, repentance, revival and restoration followed, but the word of the Lord had been fulfilled and God had shown Himself true to His promise. The cycles have continued as the years come and go, but God's faithfulness to His word remains.

The Second Regathering

Derek Prince proclaims in his book *Promised Land:*

> When I consider all the different intertwining circumstances that make this second deliverance possible, and when I take into account the diverse and numerous crises in the past century in which God sovereignly intervened to bring His prophetic Word to fulfillment, I conclude that this second deliverance is already greater than the first.[6]

What a statement, and what a fact of history!

Isaiah, God's appointed watchman, not only saw the first dispersion and regathering but also prophesied the second one. Isaiah 11:11–12 predicted that the Lord would set His hand a second time to recover a remnant of His people:

> It will happen on that day that the Lord
> Will again recover the second time with His hand
> The remnant of His people, who will remain,
> From Assyria, Egypt, Pathros, Cush, Elam, Shinar, Hamath,
> And from the islands of the sea.
> And He will lift up a standard for the nations
> And assemble the banished ones of Israel,
> And will gather the dispersed of Judah
> From the four corners of the earth.

This Scripture describes clearly a second dispersion and, at some point later, a second regathering. The first dispersion did not send these wandering Hebrews in various directions at once. They remained together as a collective entity—a very persecuted yet identifiable people in a foreign land. But the second scattering would send them to regions way beyond the known existence of Isaiah's day—out as far as the four corners of the Earth.

When did the second dispersion occur? It began around AD 70 under the Roman ruler Titus, when the Jewish people ran fearfully for their lives and fled their homeland once again. This time the Jewish people were scattered not for seventy years, not just for five hundred years or for a thousand, but for approximately 1,900 years they were banished to the four corners of the Earth.

Regarding the regathering from this second dispersion, Ramon Bennett, in his excellent book *When Day and Night Cease*, writes:

> The second gathering began with the trickle of Jews into Palestine after the turn of the last century. The trickle became a stream after 1948 and then a river during the 1950's and 1960's. The river is now in flood stage and in danger of bursting its banks with the masses arriving from the last vestiges of the [former] Soviet Union.[7]

I love it when the purposes of God unfold right in front of our eyes! From my vantage point that is exactly what is occurring in the Middle East today. It is my conviction that we are continuing to see with our very own eyes the second great regathering. The Holy Spirit is at work today breathing on God's Word, and the children of Israel are being called from the four corners of the world. Can you pierce through the clouds of confusion and see through God's prophetic lens?

People often ask me what the Lord is doing prophetically in the Earth today. I tell them about the outpouring of the Holy Spirit in South America, Africa, China and other lands. I mention the river of God's presence in various congregations, cities and nations. But I eventually always tell them about what the Lord is doing among the Jewish people worldwide.

Do you hear a trumpet blast? Do you hear what I hear? A clarion call of the purposes of God can be heard ringing clearly from Jeremiah's trumpet. Listen to the clear sound of the second great regathering:

> "Behold, I am bringing them from the north country,
> And I will gather them from the remote parts of the earth,
> Among them the blind and the lame,
> The woman with child and she who is in labor with child, together;
> A great company, they will return here.
> With weeping they will come,
> And by supplication I will lead them;
> I will make them walk by streams of waters,
> On a straight path in which they shall not stumble;
> For I am a father to Israel,
> And Ephraim is My firstborn."
> Hear the word of the LORD, O nations,
> And declare in the coastlands afar off,
> And say, "He who scattered Israel will gather him
> And keep him as a shepherd keeps his flock."
>
> Jeremiah 31:8–10

These verses paint for us a graphic picture of the painful but providential regathering process. We are even told that "the north country" will be one of the primary places of this exodus and returning.

The Lord holds the compass that points to proper interpretation of His Word. To get the correct reading, however, we must stand in the right place. To understand the regions prophesied, we must take the read from the proper geographical context. Israel is the pupil, the focal point, of God's eye, and we must read the compass of the prophetic Scriptures from this perspective. Yes indeed, the bustling city of Moscow is located directly north of the little piece of land in the Middle East that today we call Israel.

I, like many others, have ministered in "the north country"—in the former Soviet Union. I have been graced to participate in the outreach ministries of the International Festivals of Jewish Worship and Dance under the direction of Jonathan Bernis, to help lead intercessory teams for the opening of the 40/70-prayer window and to minister at other strategic events.

By June 2000, one million Jewish people had arrived in Israel from the land of the north. They fled for freedom in automobiles, airplanes, trains, buses and ships. Most were assisted by Jewish or Christian agencies, individuals and groups. It amounts to the emancipation and transportation of an entire people group from one part of the world to another. Nothing like it has ever happened on such a massive scale! But there are still far more we must reach and rescue.[8]

With well over one million Russian-speaking Jews living in Israel today, Russian is now the second-leading spoken language in the land of Israel! What a quick and sudden change happened when the walls came tumbling down!

With Weeping and Supplication

Jeremiah also predicted how God's chosen people would be led out: "With weeping they will come, and by supplication I will lead them." What is the definition of *supplication*? *Strong's*

Concordance renders the meaning of this word as "strong prayer." Jeremiah gives us the secret to the fulfillment of the prophetic promise. It is preceded by the desperate prayer of the heart (weeping) and by praying the promise back to God (supplication).

I have a challenge for all who read this book: Whose supplications will be heard? Who will lift their voices to fill up a golden bowl in heaven (see Revelation 5:8)? Will you join me?[9]

Target Practice

Now for my favorite part of the book—the part where we pray the Word of God together! As in the previous chapters, I will list prophetic Scriptures with corresponding prayers for the fullness of *aliyah* to be made complete. May the spirit of prayer and supplication come upon you, and may you lift up desperate prayers from the heart to the One who hears!

Scripture and Prayer from Psalm 126:1–2

> When the Lord brought back the captives to Zion,
> we were like men who dreamed.
> Our mouths were filled with laughter,
> our tongues with songs of joy.
> Then it was said among the nations,
> "The Lord has done great things for them."
>
> NIV

Gracious God and King, we rejoice for the day we live in! The dream of Your people returning to their own land is being fulfilled right before our very eyes! Indeed, we rejoice in the Lord and our hearts are filled with gladness. Thank You for awakening us to the prophetic reality of our times. But Lord of Hosts, we lift a cry to You, that the nations will look upon this historic event and know that there is a God in heaven! As You bring back the Jewish people from the four corners of the Earth, let the nations know that the God of the Bible is alive, and give glory to You. Indeed, the Lord has done great things and the best is yet to come! Hallelujah! Praise the Lord! Let it be!

Scripture and Prayer from Jeremiah 16:14–16

"However, the days are coming," declares the Lord, "when men will no longer say, 'As surely as the Lord lives, who brought the Israelites up out of Egypt,' but they will say, 'As surely as the Lord lives, who brought the Israelites up out of the land of the north and out of all the countries where he had banished them.' For I will restore them to the land I gave their forefathers.

"But now I will send for many fishermen," declares the Lord, "and they will catch them. After that I will send for many hunters, and they will hunt them down on every mountain and hill and from the crevices of the rocks."

NIV

Dear Lord, as we ponder on the days in which we live, we stand in awe at Your redemptive work throughout the pages of history. Demonstrate the power of Your strong arm once again and bring forth the remaining Jewish people from the land of the north into their Promised Land of Israel. Send forth many fishermen, laborers and intercessors to call them forth from all the countries where they have been scattered. Restore them to the land of their fathers as You promise in Your Word. Release a movement of signs and wonders unprecedented in all of history. Eclipse what You have done in the past and move by Your great power for Your holy name's sake! Amen.

Scripture and Prayer from Zechariah 10:8–9

I will signal for them
and gather them in.
Surely I will redeem them;

they will be as numerous as before.
Though I scatter them among the peoples,
yet in distant lands they will remember me.
They and their children will survive, and they will return.

NIV

Dear Lord, we agree with Your Word. We ask that the Holy Spirit would release a sound, an inner witness and a signal that will be recognized and acted upon by the Jewish people. Redeem Israel! Though they have been scattered, regather them from all the distant lands. Cause them to remember the one true God and to call on His name. Release divine protection to them and cause the fulfillment of aliyah *to come to pass in the Messiah's mighty name! Amen and amen!*

Aliyah: God's Last Days Mission

Our picture is nearly complete. *Aliyah*, the regathering of God's chosen people from the farthest corners of the Earth, is the great fulcrum around which He is orchestrating these final moments of history. As Israel streams back to the land, God has used *aliyah* to provoke the nations into confrontation over the increasing number of settlements in disputed territory. Eventually the land will be reclaimed, and Israel will blossom as prophesied.[10]

For the fullness of *aliyah* to come to pass, demonstrations of God's redemptive work must be completed in the land of the north, among the Sephardic Jews yet living in exile in much of Latin America, among the Jewish people of North America and among those of Europe. All eyes will end up on the Middle East. All eyes will be searching for answers as perplexing times and days of pressure mount. Leaders will be groping for answers. But God has the last word on the Middle East, because God's road map leads to Israel's future.

Reflection Questions

1. What does the term *aliyah* mean originally, and how is it commonly used today?
2. Give at least two scriptural promises concerning the return of the Jewish people to the land. Now take time to pray those promises into being!
3. Why is returning to the land so important in God's eyes? What does He promise to do when the Jewish people return to the land?

More Study Aids

Gottier, Dr. Richard F. *Aliyah, God's Last Great Act of Redemption*. Kent, England: Sovereign World Ltd., 2002.

Scheller, Gustav. *Operation Exodus*. Kent, England: Sovereign World Ltd., 1998.

9 God's Road Map for Israel's Future

> The LORD said to Abram, after Lot had separated from him, "Now lift up your eyes and look from the place where you are, northward and southward and eastward and westward; for all the land which you see, I will give it to you and to your descendants forever."
>
> Genesis 13:14–15

As I begin the last chapter of this book, I need to ask you a question: Has God rejected Israel? That may seem like an odd question to ask someone who has read so far in a book like this. But Paul did not assume that *his* audience knew the correct answer—he asked his readers, "God has not rejected His people, has he?" (Romans 11:1)—and I want to follow Paul's example for two main reasons: One, Satan has attempted to deceive the Church about Israel's destiny. Two, we cannot afford to be mistaken when it comes to the apple of God's eye.

Has God rejected Israel? Paul answered his own question, "May it never be! . . . God has not rejected His people whom He foreknew" (Romans 11:1–2).

Of course, we all would say that we agree with Paul, because reading the rest of Romans makes the question a no-brainer. A good look at the present circumstances in the Middle East and the secular opinion of our day, however, might lead us to conclude that God has rejected Israel after all.

Who could disagree with the apostle Paul? Well, the prophet Elijah might, in his time, have disagreed. Paul reminds his readers that Elijah pleaded with God *against* Israel saying, "Lord, they have killed Your prophets, they have torn down Your altars, and I alone am left, and they are seeking my life" (Romans 11:3).

But God corrected Elijah by saying, "I have kept for Myself seven thousand men who have not bowed the knee to Baal" (Romans 11:4).

Paul's point is this: Although Elijah felt alone, he was not alone. Although Israel's condition had deteriorated and her religious practices were abominable, God had saved for Himself a remnant who still walked in His ways. God wanted Elijah to know this truth, and God wanted the readers of Paul's letter, which includes you and me, to know this truth as well. Israel's circumstances today do not appear much better than they did in the time of Elijah. But the God of Israel has a road map for Israel's future, and that ultimate future is bright and glorious.

Yes, God has a plan for Israel, and His way shall prevail. The Oslo Peace Accord fell apart. The current Quartet Road Map of the European Union, United States, United Nations and Russia will eventually fail as well. Why? Because God has a road map direct from the council of His Word, and His Word shall prevail.

Speaking through the prophet Isaiah, God said, "For as the heavens are higher than the earth, so are My ways higher than your ways and My thoughts than your thoughts" (Isaiah 55:9). The Word of God will accomplish all that God desires and will succeed completely in every way He intended. God is not sitting in heaven wringing His hands, in a deep sweat from the stress and worry of the Middle East conflicts. He is not searching for a politician who can bring peace. He is the Deliverer and the Prince of Peace!

God has a road map for Israel's future, and He is looking for people on Earth who will come into agreement with Him about that plan. Will you be one who will come into agreement with God in heaven about Israel's future?

A Nation Can Be Born in a Day

The prophet Isaiah asked, "Can a land be born in one day? Can a nation be brought forth all at once?" (Isaiah 66:8). The answer is a resounding yes! Let me share a short portion from my book *Exodus Cry*:

> At one minute past midnight on May 15, 1948, the state of Israel came into being. While Israel's opponents continued to argue in the UN, they were interrupted with the announcement that U.S. President Harry S. Truman had officially recognized the new state of Israel and extended full diplomatic privileges. The USSR, eager to make sure the British never returned to the Middle East, quickly recognized the nation of Israel as well!

The descendants of Israel have undergone a journey that can hardly be described. They started as a family of seventy who traveled to Egypt to escape famine. A few hundred years later they left Egypt as a people group of over a million, feared and respected by nations all around. They were by 2,000 BC a recognized nation under King Saul and by divine right of conquest. Two generations later, Israel was one of the richest nations in eastern Asia.

Israel is the only people group—the only nation—that, after thousands of years of exile, has been brought back together by God's Word.[1] The Lord declared through the prophet Amos: "I will plant Israel in their own land, never again to be uprooted from the land I have given them" (Amos 9:15, NIV). This miracle is happening in our lifetime! You do not have to be a famous Hebrew language scholar to know that never means never! Israel is never, ever to be plucked up from her land ever again.

Four Cities of Destiny and Contention[2]

In the Six-Day War of 1967, Israel took ownership of all Jerusalem, including the Old City, for the first time since AD 70. In the last number of years, enemies of God's purposes have been attempting to force deals in which they get back land in exchange for false peace. Lies and deceptions are common, and political correctness is valued instead of the fear of God. Four important and historic sites are being bartered after as though they are poker chips that you can put on a table and say, "I'll give you this if you will do that."

Shechem, Bethel, Hebron and Jerusalem are the birthplaces of the covenants God made with Israel. God says that these covenant promises are forever (see Genesis 13:15). Many demonic and secular forces are, however, converging in an attempt to usurp and overtake these historic sites in the heartland of Israel. Muslims, other Gentile nations and some Jews are all demanding that these four places be given away to make "peace" by replacing them with an Islamic-Palestinian State. Israel's leaders offer freely to give away a rightful and highly valuable inheritance. But I want to tell you that you cannot bargain with God's Word like that.

When visiting Bethel I realized why Arafat did not want to leave the city of Ramallah, which happens to mean "the high place of Allah." Ramallah is only one minute from the city of Bethel. Bethel is the place where Israel was conceived (see Genesis 28:12–19) and born (see Genesis 35) in the person and name of Jacob, whose name was later changed to Israel. I began to realize what the enemies of Israel are trying to accomplish. They are attempting to destroy Israel's foundations and knock down the pillars at her very heart, the places where God made covenants with His people.

Islamic terrorists are among those who willfully defy God's covenants with the aim of driving the Jewish people out of their Promised Land. That is what Islamic terrorism in the Middle East is all about: uprooting and destroying God's covenant people. Their aim is none other than to push the Jews out inch by inch and to replace them with an Islamic-Palestinian State. However, in the middle of all this chaos, God's heart is to see Arabs and Jews be reconciled through the Messiah and worship Him together as a blessing in the midst of the Earth (see Isaiah 19:23–25). The following history demonstrates the biblical foundations for the case that the West Bank heartland belongs to Israel.

Shechem

When Abraham left his roots in present-day Iraq, he built his first altar of worship in Shechem. There the Lord God appeared to him and said, "To your descendants I will give this land" (Genesis 12:7). Jacob, whose name was changed to Israel in Bethel, returned to Shechem and bought the land for one hundred pieces of silver (see Genesis 33:18–19). Later Joseph's bones were brought up from Egypt to be buried in Shechem. These Scriptures show that the Jewish people have historic ownership of the area of Shechem.

Bethel

After God promised, "To your offspring I will give this land," in Shechem, Abram built an altar in nearby Bethel (see Genesis 12:8). The Lord appeared many years later to Abraham's grandson Jacob as he rested at the end of a day's journey in this same location. Genesis 28:16–19 records:

> Then Jacob awoke from his sleep and said, "Surely the Lord is in this place, and I did not know it." He was afraid and said, "How awesome is this place! This is none other than the house of God, and this is the gate of heaven." So Jacob rose early in the morning, and took the stone that he had put under his head and set it up as a pillar and poured oil on its top. He called the name of that place Bethel.

It was also at Bethel that Jacob's name was changed to Israel. God declared to Jacob, "Arise, go up to Bethel, and live there; and make an altar there to God, who appeared to you" (Genesis 35:1). So Jacob moved his entire household to Bethel, where God reaffirmed His covenant with Jacob and changed his name to Israel.

> Then God went up from him in the place where He had spoken with him. Jacob set up a pillar in the place where He had spoken with him, a pillar of stone, and he poured out a drink offering on it; he also poured oil on it. So Jacob named the place where God had spoken with him, Bethel.
>
> Genesis 35:13–15

Hebron

Abram built an altar in Hebron after he and his nephew Lot parted ways. Both Lot and Abram had many flocks, herds and tents. The land was unable to sustain them both in the same immediate area, so they agreed to separate. Lot chose the valley of Jordan; this was before the Lord destroyed Sodom and Gomorrah. After Lot had separated from Abram, the Lord encouraged Abram:

> "Now lift up your eyes and look from the place where you are, northward and southward and eastward and westward; for all the land which you see, I will give it to you and to your descendants forever. I will make your descendants as the dust of the earth, so that if anyone can number the dust of the earth, then your descendants can also be numbered. Arise, walk about the land through its length and breadth; for I will give it to you." Then Abram moved his tent and came and dwelt by the oaks of Mamre, which are in Hebron, and there he built an altar to the Lord.
>
> Genesis 13:14–18

Abraham also bought land in Hebron, the Machpelah cave, for four hundred shekels of silver (see Genesis 23:16). This cave was used as a burial site for Abraham, Sarah and their descendants. Joshua gave Hebron to Caleb as his inheritance in the Promised Land "because he followed the Lord God of Israel fully" (Joshua 14:14).

David ruled first in Hebron, for seven years. He later ruled in Jerusalem for 33 years, preparing the way for the Messiah to reign upon his throne as King of Jerusalem.

Jerusalem

The fourth Israelite city under contention today is, of course, Jerusalem. Jerusalem was the establishing place of God's ultimate covenant—the crucifixion of Jesus Christ at Golgatha. This place was known in the days of Abraham as Moriah. God told Abraham to take his son Isaac to Moriah, and to offer him as a burnt offering (see Genesis 22:1–19). This first sacrifice, the father of faith yielding up his son of promise, foreshadowed the second offering: our Father sacrificing His only Son on the same location.

It was on Mount Moriah that the Messiah, sent by *Jehovah Jireh*, "the Lord our Provider," shed His blood on the cross and opened up a new and everlasting covenant for the house of Israel (see Jeremiah 31:31).

Not only did the Messiah die and rise from the dead in Jerusalem, but He is also coming back soon to take up his throne in Jerusalem and to reign as the covenant king of this city forever. Isaiah prophesied:

> Of the increase of his government and peace
> there will be no end.
> He will reign on David's throne
> and over his kingdom,
> establishing and upholding it
> with justice and righteousness
> from that time on and forever.
>
> Isaiah 9:7, NIV

This is why Jerusalem is so significant: Jerusalem belongs to the Messiah, King of the Jews. Jerusalem is His city, to which He shall return and from which He shall reign!

Jerusalem has been politically restored to its rightful ownership, but it is still hotly contested. A demonic scheme is at work, not just to get a little Palestinian land back (as news reports would convince you to believe), but to take over the whole nation of Israel (remember Psalm 83). Under the current plan, Shechem, Bethel and Hebron will all be taken out of Jewish possession and turned over unto another stewardship.

If this happens, it will not last. There is a reason it will never last, and it is not because God loves the Jews more than He loves Arabs, Hispanics, Africans or Asians. It is because God is faithful to the promises He made to Abraham, Isaac and Jacob. God is going to demonstrate to the entire world that He is a faithful God and that the Bible is His true Word.

The Countdown to Zechariah Twelve

In January of 2004, the Lord woke me up in the middle of the night and said, *Watchman, tell me, what do you see?* I looked up and in a visionary experience saw a clock that was not there in the natural, hanging on the bedroom wall. The time on the clock read 11:53 p.m. and above the 12 were the letters "Zech." The Holy Spirit then said, *Watchman, tell me, what do you hear?* Then suddenly the external, audible voice of the Lord came: *It is the countdown to Zechariah 12.*

I rested in the presence of God for a while and did not move until His manifest presence withdrew. Then I turned on the light and read Zechariah 12. It is the most amazing chapter, all about a city named Jerusalem. Let's read a portion of it together:

> The burden of the word of the Lord concerning Israel. Thus declares the Lord who stretches out the heavens, lays the foundations of the earth, and forms the spirit of man within him, "Behold, I am going to make Jerusalem a cup that causes reeling to all the peoples around; and when the siege is against Jerusalem, it will also be against Judah. It will come about in that day that I will make Jerusalem a heavy stone for all the peoples; all who lift it will be severely injured. And all the nations of the earth will be gathered against it." . . .
>
> "In that day the Lord will defend the inhabitants of Jerusalem, and the one who is feeble among them in that day will be like David, and the house of David will be like God, like the angel of the Lord before them. And . . . I will set about to destroy all the nations that come against Jerusalem. I will pour out on the house of David and on the inhabitants of Jerusalem, the Spirit of grace and of supplication, so that they will look on Me whom they have pierced; and they will mourn for Him, as one mourns for an only son, and they will weep bitterly over Him like the bitter weeping over a firstborn."
>
> Zechariah 12:1–3, 8–10

The countdown to Zechariah 12 is on. I am not saying this will happen in the next seven minutes, seven years or seventy years. What I do know is that God's prophetic clock is moving toward a *kairos* moment when God's plan for Jerusalem will be consummated. This is the final countdown!

God has a road map, and it points toward Zechariah 12:10. It is easy to identify with Zechariah 12:3 as we hear about the nations coming against Jerusalem. But read further and you will see that Zechariah 12:10 declares that God will pour out the Spirit of grace and supplication on the house of David and the inhabitants of Jerusalem, and they will look upon the One whom they pierced and will mourn. Let's arise and pray for Israel's destiny!

Romans 11 through Isaiah 53

Since that revelatory encounter I have pondered on the time shown on the clock—11:53. Perhaps it is something like this: Romans 11 will be fulfilled through Isaiah 53. Romans 11—"all Israel will be saved"—will be fulfilled by a revelation of the Messiah in Isaiah 53.

Romans 11:12 speaks of how the Jews' rejection of their Messiah has brought salvation to the Gentiles. Paul says, "[If] their failure is riches for the Gentiles, how much more will their fulfillment be!" Romans 11:15 goes on to say, "For if their rejection is the reconciliation of the world, what will their acceptance be but life from the dead?"

What do you think "life from the dead" looks like? Zechariah 14:5, 8–9 and 11 gives us a glimpse of that day:

> Then the Lord, my God, will come, and all the holy ones with Him! . . .
>
> And in that day living waters will flow out of Jerusalem. . . .
>
> And the Lord will be king over all the earth; in that day the Lord will be the only one, and His name the only one. . . .
>
> People will live in [Jerusalem], and there will no longer be a curse, for Jerusalem will dwell in security.

The Father will reward His Son, the Messiah, for His sufferings. The salvation of Israel is a key component of that reward, and the Father will not do without it. If we are going to align ourselves with the God of Israel, we are going to have to align ourselves with His covenants and His prophetic promises of the salvation of the Jews and the restoration of Jerusalem.

It is not difficult to find political analysts, historians, reporters and even theologians ready to explain their theories and share commentary on Israel's current state of affairs. But despite the abundance of opinions and strong feelings, the future of Israel still remains a mystery to most of the world. Paul, the apostle and bond slave of the Lord Jesus Christ, did not want believers to be uninformed of this mystery or to be wise in their own estimation concerning Israel (see Romans 11:25). The Holy Spirit through Paul made a number of very clear points in Romans 11.

Despite what it may look like, Israel has not fallen so far from God that they can never return. In fact, their falling away was ordained by God as a measure of grace to us, the Gentiles. Paul said it this way: "He redeemed us in order that the blessing given to Abraham might come to the Gentiles through Christ Jesus, so that by faith we might receive the promise of the Spirit" (Galatians 3:14, NIV).

The Gentiles are being embraced by the Jewish Messiah in part to make Jews jealous (see Romans 11:11). Gentiles are not "natural branches" on God's family tree, but rather "wild olive shoots" who must recognize that they have been grafted in. God's plan is to graft the "natural branches" into their own olive tree once again (see Romans 11:24), resulting in the reality that "all Israel will be saved" (Romans 11:26).

We must not be wise in our own estimation when it comes to Israel or be uninformed of this mystery. Romans 11:25 says that "A partial hardening has happened to Israel until—"

Until what? Maybe you have read this verse many times. Have you realized that the word *until* is the key word in this passage? "A partial hardening has happened to Israel until—" That means there is a point in time when the hardening will be removed. That time is when "the fullness of the Gentiles has come in" (Romans 11:25).

What does the fullness of the Gentiles look like? Perhaps it deals in part with the day Jerusalem was released from Gentile control and restored to Israeli rule in 1967. But knowing the God that we serve, this probably does not deal only with land but with hearts as well.

What Gentile people group would, in the minds of most people, be the most unlikely to come to faith in the Jewish Messiah? Would it not be the Islamic people? What if the Holy Spirit moved powerfully upon a remnant of the Islamic people and they turned away from their false god to serve the Jewish Messiah? What if a movement of God fell upon them with the signs and wonders of an apostolic dimension, and they were grafted in as wild olive shoots to the Master's tree? Talk about pricking the Jewish heart to jealousy!

All I know is that God has a road map, and His will shall be done.

Target Practice

It is time for our last Target Practice! I hope that by the time you have finished this book your times of intercession will no longer be just practice sessions, but they will be impact sessions! That is my goal but, for now, let's get in one more shot!

Scripture and Prayer from Isaiah 55:6–9

Seek the LORD while He may be found;
Call upon Him while He is near.
Let the wicked forsake his way
And the unrighteous man his thoughts;
And let him return to the LORD,
And He will have compassion on him;
And to our God,
For He will abundantly pardon.

"For My thoughts are not your thoughts,
Nor are your ways My ways," declares the Lord.
"For as the heavens are higher than the earth,
So are My ways higher than your ways
And My thoughts than your thoughts."

Lord, Your ways are higher than our ways. Your thoughts are higher than our thoughts. Let us know Your ways and think Your thoughts concerning Israel. Open the eyes of the hearts of Your people Israel so that they see You as the One they have been waiting for. I ask that Israel would seek You with all of their hearts. I thank You for Your promise that You will be found by those who seek You. I ask that Israel's encounter with the Messiah would cause the wicked to forsake their own way and the unrighteous all their evil thoughts. I call out to Israel, "Come and return to the Lord. He will have compassion on you and pardon your sins." Thank You for Your mercy and kindness and Your willingness to abundantly pardon those who turn to You. In the name of the Lord, amen.

Scripture and Prayer from Amos 9:14–15

"Also I will restore the [fortunes] of My people Israel,
And they will rebuild the ruined cities and live in them;
They will also plant vineyards and drink their wine,
And make gardens and eat their fruit.
I will also plant them on their land,
And they will not again be rooted out from their land
Which I have given them,"
Says the Lord your God.

Father, restore the wealth of Your people, Israel. I agree with You that they will rebuild ruined cities and live in them, plant vineyards, make gardens and eat their fruit. Bring Israel's time of barrenness to an end and let them bear fruit for Your Kingdom. Thank You that Israel is being replanted in their land. I call forth righteous leaders who will recognize Israel, reach out to Israel in relationship and stand with her. Thank You for Your Word which promises that the people of Israel will never again be uprooted from their land. Stir the people of Israel to possess their full inheritance—the land promised to their forefathers. With thanksgiving and praise, through Your Son, the Messiah. Amen.

Scripture and Prayer from Zechariah 12:8–10

In that day the Lord will defend the inhabitants of Jerusalem, and the one who is feeble among them in that day will be like David, and the house of David will be like God, like the angel of the Lord before them. And in that day I will set about to destroy all the nations that come against Jerusalem. I will pour out on the house of David and on the inhabitants of Jerusalem, the Spirit of grace and of supplication, so that they will look on Me whom they have pierced; and they will mourn for Him, as one mourns for an only son, and they will weep bitterly over Him, like the bitter weeping over a firstborn.

Lord God, I thank You that a day is coming when You will defend the inhabitants of Your city, Jerusalem. Hasten that day, Lord! Stretch out Your mighty hand and strengthen the weak. Pour out upon the house of David and all the inhabitants of Jerusalem Your Spirit of grace and supplication. Open their eyes to see the One our sin has pierced. Prick their hearts. I ask that godly sorrow would draw them to repentance and faith in Your holy Son, their elder brother, Yeshua. *Amen.*

God's Plan Includes You

The story of Israel is all about a God who keeps His promises. In my lifetime I have seen a nation born in one day, restored never to be plucked out again. From this point of restoration, God's road map calls for a body of believers, with the spirit of Mordecai and Esther, to carry God's heart for such a time as this.

The road leads to Romans 11, and it goes through Isaiah 53. It is the salvation of all Israel through the revelation of their suffering Servant. When Israel is grafted back in, it will be nothing less than life from the dead. When we labor for Israel, we are laboring for the greatest worldwide outpouring of the Holy Spirit that there has ever been.

Our God is the holy Lord of heaven, and His Word never fails. He is the judge of all, living and dead, and has the final word on your life and on the Middle East. But He is looking for a people who will come into agreement with Him.

Will we allow these four places of covenant foundation—these pillars of the house of Israel—to be toppled by Islam, or will we take a stand and agree with the covenant God of Israel even, if necessary, against all odds? We are children of Abraham by faith. We have been bought with the price of *Yeshua*'s covenant blood. We belong to the High and Holy One who inhabits eternity and who is the King of Jerusalem. Will you take a stand? God is looking for allies—will you be one?

In the first chapter of this book, I called for a yearly prayer thrust called The Cry. Are you willing to give your life, like Esther and Mordecai, as a sacrifice for God's purposes? God has a purpose and a plan for every person, family, city and nation! Indeed the Lord of Hosts has a great destiny for Israel and all the nations of the Middle East.

Believe it? Then join me and countless thousands of others, and let's pray these promises into being! Indeed, God has a plan and a glorious future for Israel. Join me now in this closing prayer of dedication.

Father God, it was for such a time as this that I have come into Your Kingdom. If I die, I die, for my life is but a gift from You and is not my own. Place Your mighty hand upon me to be a Mordecai that helps the Esthers, to be a forerunner voice crying in the wilderness. Let a people arise who will cry out for the destiny of Israel and intercede effectively for Your purposes in the

Middle East. As for me and my house, I want to be possessed by You for Your purposes. Come, Lord, and do this for Your name's sake, that You may receive the reward for Your sufferings on behalf of all Jews and Gentiles alike. I dedicate myself into Your grace and for Your purposes. Amen and amen!

Reflection Questions

1. Name the four cities mentioned in this chapter over which there is great conflict today. Why is there such conflict over them?
2. Recite Zechariah 12:10 and now take time to pray that verse.
3. What were the roles of Mordecai and Esther as stated in the book of Esther, and how do their lives relate to the days in which we live?

More Study Aids

Intrater, Keith and Dan Juster. *Israel, the Church, and the Last Days*. Shippensburg, Pa.: Destiny Image, 2003.

Facius, Johannes. *Hastening the Coming of the Messiah*. Kent, England: Sovereign World Ltd., 2001.

Appendix: The Cry Yearly Prayer Focus

While under the reign of Persia's King Artaxerxes, Queen Esther called for a three-day fast with intercession for crisis intervention on behalf of her Jewish people nationwide. She entered the throne room of her king on the third day of her fast (see Esther 4:16–5:1) to make her bold and righteous appeal. With the same heart for the Jewish people, we are calling for an annual time of seeking the face of God for the overthrowing of evil in our day.

Purim is a Jewish holiday celebrated each year in memory of God's intervention as a result of Esther's intercession. The holiday was held the fourteenth day of Adar (according to the Jewish calendar) in the unwalled cities and on the fifteenth day in the cities that were walled during the time of Joshua. (For more details read *Exodus Cry* by James W. Goll, available at http://www.encountersnetwork.com.) The following is a listing of the dates for the Feast of Purim and The Cry Prayer Focus for the next several years.

Year	Feast of Purim	The Cry Prayer Focus
2005	March 25	March 23–25
2006	March 14	March 12–14
2007	March 4	March 2–4
2008	March 21	March 19–21
2009	March 10	March 8–10
2010	February 28	February 26–28
2011	March 20	March 18–20
2012	March 8	March 6–8
2013	February 24	February 22–24
2014	March 16	March 14–16
2015	March 5	March 3–5
2016	March 24	March 22–24
2017	March 12	March 10–12
2018	March 1	February 27–March 1
2019	March 21	March 19–21
2020	March 10	March 8–10

Notes

Chapter 1: Appointed a Watchman for Israel

1. Jim W. Goll, *Intercession* (Shippensburg, Pa.: Destiny Image, 2003), 15.

2. Jim W. Goll, *Kneeling on the Promises* (Grand Rapids, Mich.: Chosen Books, 1999), 185.

3. Johannes Facius, *Hastening the Coming of the Messiah* (Kent, England: Sovereign World Ltd., 2001), 14.

4. Jim W. Goll, *Exodus Cry* (Ventura, Calif.: Regal Books, 2001), 176–177.

5. Ibid., 182.

Chapter 2: Character to Carry the Burden

1. Samuel J. Schultz, *The Old Testament Speaks,* 3rd ed. (San Francisco: Harper & Row, 1980), 255, 268. This is used as a reference but not directly quoted.

Chapter 3: A Heart Like These

1. Norman L. Geisler, *A Popular Survey of the Old Testament* (Grand Rapids, Mich.: Baker Book House, 1977), 235–236. This is used as a reference but not directly quoted.

2. Ibid., 243.

3. Samuel J. Schultz, *The Old Testament Speaks,* 3rd ed. (San Francisco: Harper & Row, 1980), 323. This is used as a reference but not directly quoted.

4. Geisler, 264.

5. Schultz, 323–343.

6. Ibid., 365.

Chapter 4: The Descendants of Hagar

1. Sandra Teplinsky, *Why Care About Israel?* (Grand Rapids, Mich.: Chosen Books, 2004), 161.

2. Avner Boskey, *A Perspective on Islam* (Nashville, Tenn.: Final Frontier Ministries, 2001), 16.

Chapter 5: The Descendants of Sarah

1. Sandra Teplinsky, *Why Care About Israel?* (Grand Rapids, Mich.: Chosen Books, 2004), 84–85.

2. Ibid., 85.

3. Ibid., 84.

4. Derek Prince, *Promised Land, God's Word and the Nation of Israel* (Charlotte, N.C.: Derek Prince Ministries, 2003), 17–18.

5. Asher Intrater quoted in Ari and Shira Sorko-Ram, *Praying for Israel: How?* (Tel Aviv, Israel: Maoz Israel Report, 2004), 2. Visit http://www.revive-israel.org for more on this article and subject.

6. Ibid., 2.

7. Ibid.

8. Kai Kje-Hasen, *Joseph Rabinowitz and the Messianic Movement: The Herzl of Jewish Christianity* (Grand Rapids, Mich.: Wm. B. Eerdman's Publishing Co.; The Stables, Carberry, Scotland: The Handsel Press LTD; 1995), 18–19.

9. Don Finto, *Your People Shall Be My People* (Ventura, Calif.: Regal Books, 2001). For more on the subject of the modern day Messianic Movement, I commend to you this outstanding book.

Chapter 6: The Descendants of Keturah

1. Sandra Teplinsky, *Why Care About Israel?* (Grand Rapids, Mich.: Chosen Books, 2004), 237.

2. Ibid.

3. Robert Somerville, *The Three Families of Abraham* (Huntsville, Ala.: Awareness Ministry, 2002). Though I have not quoted directly from this book, this short manuscript was placed in my hands at just the right moment and its contents were very helpful in the penning of chapters 4, 5 and 6.

Chapter 7: Jerusalem: A City of Destiny

1. Barry Segal and Batya Segal, *Jerusalem—On-The-Line* (Jerusalem, Israel: Vision for Israel, 2004). This portion was taken from the monthly prayer letter via the Internet on May 27, 2004.

2. Mike Evans, *Jerusalem Prayer Team* (Euless, Tex.: Jerusalem Prayer Team, 2004). Inspiration for this section and a direct quotation were taken from the weekly newsletter via the Internet. For more information visit http://www.jerusalemprayerteam.org.

3. Michael D. Evans, *The American Prophecies* (New York: Time Warner Books, 2004), 85–86.

4. Ibid., 87.

5. Ibid., 97.

6. Mike Evans, *Jerusalem Prayer Team* (Euless, Tex.: Jerusalem Prayer Team, 2004). Inspiration for this section and a direct quotation were taken from the weekly newsletter via the Internet. For more information visit http://www.jerusalemprayerteam.org.

7. Ruth Ward Heflin, *Jerusalem, Zion, Israel and the Nations* (Hagertown, Md.: McDougal Publishing, 1999), 4–16. This book was used as a reference for this chapter, although I took no direct quotations.

8. Ibid., 19–30; 47–48; 53–57.

9. Johannes Facius, *Hastening the Coming of the Messiah* (Kent, England: Sovereign World Ltd., 2001), 84.

10. Ibid., 85.

11. Robert Stearns, "Prayer for the Peace of Jerusalem," *Kairos Magazine* (Clarence, N.Y.: Kairos Publishing, 2003), 8–9.

12. Robert Stearns and Jack Hayford, "Day of Prayer," http://www.daytopray.com (August 2004).

Chapter 8: Praying for the Fulfillment of *Aliyah*

1. Dr. Richard F. Gottier, *Aliyah, God's Last Great Act of Redemption* (Kent, England: Sovereign World Ltd., 2002), 10.

2. Tom Hess, *Let My People Go!* (Washington, D.C.: Progressive Vision, 1987), 118–120.

3. Malcom Hedding, *Understanding Israel* (Oklahoma City, Okla.: Zion's Gate International, 2002), 145.

4. Ibid., 19.

5. James W. Goll, *Kneeling on the Promises* (Grand Rapids, Mich.: Chosen Books, 1999). The contents of this chapter were shaped by the same truths that I searched out while writing my earlier book.

6. Derek Prince, *Promised Land, God's Word and the Nation of Israel* (Charlotte, N.C.: Derek Prince Ministries, 2003), 75–76.

7. Ramon Bennett, *When Day and Night Cease* (Jerusalem, Israel: Arm of Salvation, 1992), 122–123.

8. James W. Goll, *Exodus Cry* (Ventura, Calif.: Regal Books, 2001), 107–108.

9. Ibid., 182.

10. Gottier, 89.

Chapter 9: God's Road Map for Israel's Future

1. Gordon Lindsay, *The Miracle of Israel* (Dallas: Christ for the Nations, Inc., 1987), 46.

2. Tom Hess, untitled teaching material (Jerusalem, Israel: Jerusalem House of Prayer for All Nations, 2003), 1–2. Portions of this section were drawn from the teaching ministry of Tom Hess.

Glossary

I trust this simple glossary of terms will help clarify the meaning of a few terms I have used throughout this book. This is by no means a thorough and comprehensive professional dictionary. Rather, I have simply defined a few terms in my own words. I hope this will be of help to you, thus making the book a bit more reader and user friendly.

***Aliyah*:** The Hebrew word for the return of the Jews to their homeland in Israel. It literally means "going up."

Anti-Semitism/Anti-Semitic: Intense dislike, hostility, hatred or discrimination against Jewish people, religious practices, culture or ethnicity.

Day of Atonement: The most holy day for the Jews, an annual day of fasting, penitence and sacrifice for sin. Before the destruction of the Temple, the high priest would enter the Holy of Holies on the tenth day of the seventh month of the Hebrew calendar and offer sacrifices for the sanctuary, the priests and the people. This foreshadowed the entrance of Jesus, the great High Priest, who offered Himself as the eternal sacrifice once for all, having purchased for us eternal salvation. This day, also known as Yom Kippur, is observed today with fasting and confession of sins.

Diaspora: A dispersion of the Jews from their homeland, such as the Jewish people being sent into Egypt in the time of Moses.

Fasting: To abstain from food as a sacrifice unto God for spiritual release of power and intervention. Also an act of humbling one's soul before God.

Gentile: This Hebrew word literally means "nations," but it is used to describe any person who is neither of Jewish origin nor an adherent of Judaism.

Harp and Bowl: This is a term taken from Revelation 5 and 8, describing "worship and intercession." The harp symbolically represents worship, and the bowl filled with incense is a description of the prayers of believers. Therefore, the term "harp and bowl" is often used to describe the combined activities of worship and intercession.

Holocaust: It is the name given to the most tragic period of the second Jewish exile. It spans twelve years from 1933–1945. It was the Nazi-inspired "final solution" to the so-called Jewish problem, and it called for the systematic destruction of the Jewish people. It is estimated that at least six million Jews died in this tragic period.

Identificational Repentance: This is a form of intercession in which one confesses the generational sins of the family, ethnic group, city and/or nation of one's background. The intercessor discerns the generational iniquity of his or her family and/or people group and thus repents before God for this sin or injustice. For more on this subject, read my book *Intercession: The Power and the Passion to Shape History.*

Intercession: The act of making a request to a superior, or expressing a deep-seated yearning to our one and only superior, God.

Intercessor: One who reminds God of His promises and appointments yet to be fulfilled; who takes up a case of injustice before God on behalf of another; who makes up the "hedge" (that is, builds up the wall in time of battle); and who stands in the gap between God's righteous judgments and the people's need for mercy.

Kairos: There are two different Greek New Testament words used to describe the word "time." *Chronos* is the Greek word describing the chronology of ordered events. *Kairos* is used to describe when time and promise meet, creating a "strategic time" when God's plans, purposes and destiny unfold in that specific moment.

Olim: Those going up from other lands.

Land of the North: This Old Testament term is used to describe those regions geographically located directly north of Jerusalem. This term especially is used to describe the region of the former Soviet Union. For more on this subject, please read my book *Exodus Cry*.

Prophet/Prophetess: A man or woman who represents the interests of God to the people. Having stood in the council of God, the prophet releases a clarion call to the people of what is in God's heart at the moment. Some refer to this as one of the fivefold ministry gifts listed in Ephesians 4:11.

Prophetic Intercession: The act of waiting before God in order to hear or receive His burden—His word, concern, warning, condition, vision or promise—and responding back to Him and the people with appropriate actions.

Sephardic/Sephardim: Sephard means "Spain" in Hebrew. Thus the term refers to the Jewish people of Spanish and/or Portuguese origin or descent. Many Sephardic Jews live in Central and South America today.

Supplication: To entreat, seek, implore or beseech God in earnest prayer.

Travail: The prayer that brings forth a birthing in the spirit, which creates or enlarges an opening for an increased dimension of the Kingdom of God.

Visitation: A supernatural experience in which a distinct sense of the presence of God is accompanied by fear of the Lord. This may come in the form of an angelic visitation, as in the book of Acts, or by other biblical means.

Watch of the Lord: A gathering in Jesus' name (see Matthew 24; Mark 13; Luke 21) to watch, pray and be vigilant for the life of a church, city or nation. It is also a position on the wall of the Lord in order to see outside the city, in order to alert the gatekeepers of approaching enemies or envoys from the King, and inside the city to recognize and confront disorderly, unlawful activity of the enemy within.

Watchmen: Those who serve in the position of watching. See "watch of the Lord."

***Yeshua*:** This is the Hebrew or Jewish word used to describe Jesus Christ the Messiah—the one who saves.

Zionism: The movement birthed by Theodor Herzl in the late 1800s in Switzerland believing the true destiny of the Jewish people could only be found in a national home of their own, in Zion, their ancient covenant home. These "Zionists" urged the Jewish people to flee Europe and return to their ancient homeland in the Middle East for decades before the holocaust began.

Referral Ministries

There are numerous wonderful ministries emphasizing prayer, worship and fasting; compassion, outreach and humanitarian aid; inspirational teaching and reconciliation events and rallies; return of the Jewish people or *aliyah* to the land; etc., for Israel and the Jewish people worldwide. The following are but a few of these ministries.

Prayer Ministries

Jerusalem House of Prayer for All Nations

Tom Hess is the Director of the Jerusalem House of Prayer for All Nations in Jerusalem, Israel. For more information on the numerous prayer convocations held yearly and their weekly prayer ministry in Israel, contact jhopfan@compuserve.com.

Jerusalem Prayer Team

Chaired by Mike Evans of Euless, Texas, the Jerusalem Prayer Team is calling for one million people to join in regular prayer for God's purposes to be fulfilled in Israel. For more information, visit http://www.jerusalemprayerteam.org.

Prayer for the Peace of Jerusalem Day

Prayer for the Peace of Jerusalem emphasis across the global Body of Christ is the first Sunday in October each year. The *Resolution for a Call to Prayer* quoted in chapter 7 is promoted by Eagles' Wings Ministries and others. For more information, visit: http://www.daytopray.com, composed under the leadership of Robert Stearns and Jack Hayford.

The Cry—Purim Prayer Thrust

For information on this annual three days of prayer and fasting during the season of Purim, read the book *Exodus Cry* by James W. Goll. Visit http://www.encountersnetwork.com and view the Israel Acts section for reports and updates on this prayer strategy. Also see the appendix in this book for dates of this yearly Esther-like emphasis.

The Elijah Prayer Army—Weekly Prayer Emails

Lars Enarson is the director ofThe Watchman International with an emphasis calling for special times of fasting and prayer each Friday especially for intervention in the Muslim and Jewish conflict. To sign up for the Elijah Prayer Army and receive their prayer alerts, do so at epa@thewatchman.org. A yearly Passover prayer convocation is coordinated. For more information, contact www.thewatchman.org.

United Prayer Coalition—Monthly Prayer Guide

United Prayer Coalition, initially formed by Aglow International, Lydia Fellowship and Endtime Handmaidens, provides a Prayer Guide of 31 Daily Scripture Prayers for America, Israel and the Youth. To view or download this strategic prayer tool, visit the Prayer Storm section of http://www.encountersnetwork.com.

Humanitarian Aid

Israel Relief Fund

The Israel Relief Fund, working in conjunction with other ministries, sends humanitarian aid to the poor in Israel and sends goods to third world countries on behalf of Israel. For more information, visit the web site at http://www.israelrelief.org or call 1-615-742-5500.

Vision for Israel & The Joseph Storehouse

Vision for Israel has the privilege of being a conduit for a "flow of the spirit" that touches the hearts and lives of our fellow man living in the nations of Israel through tangible means. For more information, contact http://www

.visionforisrael.com or email info@visionforisrael.com. Barry and Batya Segal are the directors of this ministry.

Education, Reconciliation and Media

Jewish Voice Ministries International

Directed by Jonathan Bernis, JVMI is a worldwide outreach that shares the Gospel with the Jew first, and also the nations through television, radio, publishing and large-scale Messianic Outreach Festivals. For more information, contact www.jewishvoicetoday.org.

Messianic Vision

As president of Messianic Vision, a nationally syndicated radio, television and publishing ministry, Sid Roth has been on the cutting edge of Jewish evangelism for more than 25 years. An archive of Sid's radio and television programs can be found at www.sidroth.org.

Road to Jerusalem

A newly formed ministry by Coach Bill McCarthy, founder of Promise Keepers, emphasizes teaching, education and encouragement for the Gentile church to return to her Jewish roots through rallies and events. Interaction, reconciliation and fellowship is fostered with the Messianic Jew portion of the Body of Christ. For more information, visit www.roadtojerusalem.org.

Toward Jerusalem Council II—Jew and Gentile Reconciliation

Toward Jerusalem Council II is an initiative of repentance and reconciliation between the Jewish and Gentile segments of the Church working toward the biblical expression of the "one new man." For more information, contact Marty Waldman, executive general secretary, at egs@tjc2.org.

Aliyah—Return to the Land Emphasis

Ebenezer House—Return of the Jewish People to the Land

This ministry raises funds to help Jewish people make *aliyah* by ship and by plane back to Israel. It was founded by Gustav Scheller and Johannes Facius. For more information, contact the Ebenezer House at ecf@btinternet.com.

Exobus Project

This ministry operates a fleet of buses to help transport Jewish people making *aliyah* from their homes in other countries to major airports, ports or transportation hubs where other coordinated transportation awaits them. For information, contact them at exobus@exobus.org.

Recommended Reading

Alves, Elizabeth. *Discovering Your Prayer Power.* Ventura, Calif.: Regal Books, 2001.

Archbold, Norma. *The Mountains of Israel.* Jerusalem, Israel: Phoebe's Song Publication, 1993.

Bennett, Ramon. *When Day and Night Cease.* Jerusalem, Israel: Arm of Salvation, 1992.

Brimmer, Rebecca J. *"For Zion's Sake I Will Not Be Silent."* Jerusalem, Israel: Bridges for Peace International, 2003.

Brown, Michael L. *Our Hands Are Stained with Blood.* Shippensburg, Pa.: Destiny Image, 1992.

Evans, Michael D. *The American Prophecies.* New York: Time Warner Books, 2004.

Facius, Johannes. *As in the Days of Noah.* Tonbridge, England: Sovereign World Ltd., 1997.

———. *Hastening the Coming of the Messiah.* Kent, England: Sovereign World Ltd., 2001.

Finto, Don. *Your People Shall Be My People.* Ventura, Calif.: Regal Books, 2001.

Goll, James W. *Exodus Cry.* Ventura, Calif.: Regal Books, 2001.

———. *Intercession.* Shippensburg, Pa.: Destiny Image, 2003.

———. *Kneeling on the Promises.* Grand Rapids, Mich.: Chosen Books, 1999.

———. *Prayers for Israel* CD and audiotape. Kelowna, British Columbia, Canada: Revival Now! Resources, 1999. (This may be ordered from Encounters Network website at http://www.encountersnetwork.com.)

Gottier, Dr. Richard F. *Aliyah, God's Last Great Act of Redemption.* Kent, England: Sovereign World Ltd., 2002.

Hedding, Malcom. *Understanding Israel.* Oklahoma City, Okla.: Zion's Gate International, 2002.

Hess, Tom. *Let My People Go!* Washington, D.C.: Progressive Vision, 1987.

———. *The Watchmen: Being Prepared and Preparing the Way for Messiah.* Washington, D.C.: Progressive Vision International, 1998.

Heflin, Ruth Ward. *Jerusalem, Zion, Israel and the Nations.* Hagerstown, Md.: McDougal Publishing, 1999.

Intrater, Keith and Dan Juster. *Israel, the Church, and the Last Days.* Shippensburg, Pa.: Destiny Image, 2003.

Juster, Dan. *Jewish Roots.* Shippensburg, Pa.: Destiny Image, 1995.

Kjaer-Hansen, Kai. *Joseph Rabinowitz and the Messianic Movement.* Grand Rapids, Mich.: Wm. B. Eerdman's Publishing Co. and The Stables, Carberry, Scotland: The Handsel Press Ltd., 1995.

Lambert, Lance. *Battle for Israel.* Eastbourne, England: Kingsway Publications, 1976.

———. *The Uniqueness of Israel.* Eastbourne, England: Kingsway Publications, 1991.

Lindsay, Gordon. *The Miracle of Israel.* Dallas: Christ for the Nations, Inc., 1987.

Prince, Derek. *Praying for the Government.* Fort Lauderdale, Fla.: Derek Prince Ministries, 1970.

———. *Shaping History through Prayer and Fasting.* Old Tappan, N.J.: Spire, 1973.

———. *The Last Word on the Middle East.* Lincoln, Va.: Chosen, 1978.

———. *Promised Land, God's Word and the Nation of Israel.* Charlotte, N.C.: Derek Prince Ministries, 2003.

Scheller, Gustav. *Operation Exodus.* Kent, England: Sovereign World Ltd., 1998.

Somerville, Robert. *The Three Families of Abraham.* Huntsville, Ala.: Awareness Ministry, 2002.

Teplinsky, Sandra. *Out of Darkness: The Untold Story of Jewish Revival in the Former Soviet Union.* Jacksonville Beach, Fla.: Hear O Israel Publishing, 1998.

———. *Why Care About Israel?* Grand Rapids, Mich.: Chosen Books, 2004.

Williamson, Clyde and James Craig. *The Esther Mandate Fast.* Toronto, Ontario, Canada: Almond Publications, 1987.

For More Information

James (Jim) W. Goll is the cofounder of Encounters Network (formerly Ministry to the Nations) with his wife, Michal Ann. He is a member of the Harvest International Ministries Apostolic Team and serves on numerous national and international councils. He is also a contributing writer for *Kairos* magazine and other periodicals.

James and Michal Ann have four wonderful children and live in the beautiful rolling hills of Franklin, Tennessee.

James has produced several study guides on subjects such as Equipping in the Prophetic, Blueprints for Prayer and Empowered for Ministry. Hundreds of audio teaching tapes and CDs and numerous video recordings are also available through the Encounters Resource Center.

Other books by Jim W. and Michal Ann Goll:

The Lost Art of Intercession
Kneeling on the Promises
Fire On the Altar
Wasted on Jesus

Exodus Cry
Elijah's Revolution
The Coming Prophetic Revolution
Women on the Frontlines—A Call to Courage
Intercession: The Power and the Passion to Shape History
A Call to the Secret Place
The Beginner's Guide to Hearing God
The Seer
God Encounters

For more information contact:

Encounters Network
P. O. Box 1653
Franklin, TN 37075

Office Phone: 615-599-5552
Office Fax: 615-599-5554
For orders call: 1-877-200-1604
Email: info@encountersnetwork.com

For information about conferences, product resources or to sign up for monthly email Communiqués, visit www.jamesgoll.com or www.encountersnetwork.com.

In *Exodus Cry*, Jim W. Goll traces God's plan—as prophesied in the Bible—to bring millions of Jewish people out from under persecution in the land of the North. The Great Exodus from the North has already begun—a movement that will lead to the eyes of Israel opening at last to see their Messiah! The Church is called to carry them home on the shoulders of prayer.

Index

Abraham, 48, 59, 75, 89
  and Hagar, 63–73
  at Hebron, 144–45
  and Keturah, 91–96
  and Sarah, 77–89
  at Shechem, 143
Adonijah, 32
Africa, 133
Aglow International, 166
aliyah, 123–24, 127, 129, 135, 137, 161, 167
Amalek, 98
Ammon, 98
Amos, 142
anti-Semitism, 161
Arabia, 98
Arabs, 69, 70–71, 75, 94, 112, 125
Artaxerxes, 34, 155
Asaph, 35–37
Asia Minor, 95
Assyria, 72, 95, 98
Athaliah, 46
atheism, 113
Auschwitz, 109

Babylonian captivity, 51, 83, 129–31
Bathsheba, 32
beasts of burden, 29–30, 42–43, 45, 59
Ben-Gurion, David, 125
Bennett, Ramon, 132
Bernis, Jonathan, 134, 167
Bethel, 142–44, 146
Bickle, Mike, 45
blessing of nations, 69–73
Boskey, Avner, 14, 75, 108
Boskey, Rachel, 14
burden-bearing. See beasts of burden

chaos, 95
character, 30, 37–38, 46, 59
China, 133
Christians, in Jerusalem, 108
Churchill, Winston, 112
circumcision, 66, 67–68, 80
City of David, 114
communism, 113
compassion, for Israel, 17–18, 23
covenant, 31, 65–66, 67, 71, 142–43, 145–46, 149
cross, 118
Crusade, 109
Cry, The, 24–25, 153, 155–56, 166
Cyrus the Persian, 52

Dachau concentration camp, 110
Daniel, 51–53, 129–31
Darius the Mede, 52
darkness, 95, 96–97, 98, 110
David, 32, 45, 115, 145
Day of Atonement, 161
Diaspora, 129, 162
discernment, 32

Eagles' Wings Ministries, 121, 166
Ebenezer Emergency Fund International, 22
Ebenezer House, 167
Edom, 97
Egypt, 30–31, 94–95, 96, 97, 126, 141
Elijah, 140
Elijah Prayer Army, 166
El Shaddai, 77
Enarson, Lars, 166
Endtime Handmaidens, 166
Ephah, 93
Esau, 81
Esther, 24, 152, 153, 155
Europe, 137, 140
Evans, Mike, 165
exile, 109, 129–31
Exobus Project, 167
Ezekiel, 129

Facius, Johannes, 22–23, 167
faith, 80
fasting, 24, 31, 47, 162
Final Frontier Ministries, 14, 75, 108
frankincense, 93

Gabriel, 52
Gaza Strip, 98, 126
Gebal, 98
Gentiles, 149–50, 162
Germany, 97
Giuliani, Rudolph, 113
God
  compassion, 23, 47
  covenant, 48, 71, 84, 142–43
  faithfulness, 84, 127, 129, 146
  glory, 32
  heart, 71, 73
  mercy, 49
  road map, 148, 150
  vision, 15
Goetz, Marty, 108
Golan Heights, 126
gold, 93
Goll, James W., 166
grace, 98

Hagar, 64, 65, 68–69, 82, 94, 96
Hagrites, 97
harp and bowl, 36, 37, 162
Hayford, Jack, 121, 166
healing, 118, 128
heart, 45–46, 59
Hebron, 142, 144–45, 146
Hedding, Malcolm, 128
Herzl, Theodore, 164
Hess, Tom, 165
history, 110
Hitler, Adolf, 110, 124
Holocaust, 109, 110–11, 124, 162
Holy Spirit, 24–25, 59, 95, 149
holy war, 96, 125
hope, 47, 99
Hosea, 128
human rights, 111
humility, 47

identificational repentance, 131, 162
intercession, 131, 155, 162
International Christian Embassy Jerusalem, 128
International Day of Prayer for the Peace of Jerusalem, 120–22
International Festivals of Jewish Worship and Dance, 134
Intrater, Asher, 85
Iran, 95, 102
Iraq, 95, 96, 98, 102, 126
Isaac, 67–68, 78–79, 80, 81, 84, 86, 93, 145
Isaiah, 47–49, 94, 140, 141
Ishmael, 63, 66–73, 75, 82, 93
Ishmaelites, 97
Islam, 75–76, 96, 143, 150, 153
Israel
  acceptance of Messiah, 22
  apple of God's eye, 15, 16, 71, 140

restoration, 127–31
salvation, 19–20, 148
second regathering, 131–33
statehood, 84, 111, 125–26, 141
Israel (name), 82
Israel Prayer Watch, 19, 64, 102
Israel Relief Fund, 21, 166
Israeli War of Independence, 126
Israelite, 83

Jacob, 67, 81–82, 143, 144
Jeremiah, 49–51, 84, 127, 133, 134–35
Jerusalem, 18, 20, 107–22, 145–46
after Six-Day War, 142
destruction of, 50
names for, 113–14
prayer for, 120–22
restoration of, 34–35, 131, 149
and U.S. State Department, 111–12
Jerusalem Center for Israel Research, 108
Jerusalem Embassy Act, 112, 113
Jerusalem House of Prayer for All Nations, 165
Jerusalem Prayer Team, 165
Jesus
crucifixion, 145–46
as Prince of Peace, 118
second coming, 22–23, 146
as seed of Abraham, 71
Jew (term), 67, 83
Jewish Voice Ministries International (JVMI), 167
Jews, 83–84
in Jerusalem, 108, 109
jihad, 125
Joash, 46
Joel, 46–47
Jonah, 48, 49
Jordan, 97, 98, 126
Joseph Storehouse, The, 21, 166
Judah, 67, 83
judgment, 128
justice, 32

kairos, 147, 162–63
Kedar, 72
Keturah, 91–96, 100, 102

Laban, 81
Lamentations, 50
land covenant, 84–85
"land of the heart", 85–86
land of the north, 97, 134, 137, 163
Latin America, 137
laughter, 80
League of Nations, 124
Lebanon, 96, 98, 126
light, 98–99
Long, Breckenridge, 110
Lot, 144
Lydia Fellowship, 166

Maccabees, 24
Marshall, George C., 111
McCarthy, Bill, 167
Messiah, 22, 48, 83, 86, 93–94, 101, 118
Messianic Vision, 167
Middle East, 85, 94–95, 102, 117, 133–34, 137, 141
Midian, 92, 93
Moab, 97
Mohammed, 101
Mordecai, 24, 152, 153
Moriah, 145
Moscow, 134
Moses, 30–32, 37
Mount Sinai, 31
Muslims, 108, 109, 142

Nazi Germany, 124
Nebaioth, 72
Nebuchadnezzar, 51, 130
Nehemiah, 34–35
Nineveh, 48
North America, 134

Old City (Jerusalem), 142
olim, 163
order, out of chaos, 95
Orr, William W., 129
Oslo Peace Accord, 117, 140

Palestine, 124
Palestinians, 71, 125
Palestinian State, 142, 143, 146
Palm Sunday, 29, 42

peace, 117–19
Peace of Jerusalem, 20, 117–19, 120–21
Persia, 34, 93, 96
Philistia, 98
prayer, 24, 47
    for Israel, 17–19
Prayer for the Peace of Jerusalem Day, 166
Prince, Derek, 83, 129, 131
prophetic intercession, 17, 130–31, 163
prophets, 46–53, 163
Psalms, 36–37, 114–15, 124
Purim, 24, 155–56, 166

Quartet Road Map, 117, 140

Rabinowitz, Joseph, 85–86
Rachel, 81
Ramallah, 142
Rebekah, 81
repentance, 47
revival, 22, 101
Ridings, Rick, 71
Road to Jerusalem, 167
Roosevelt, Franklin D., 110
Roth, Sid, 167
Russia, 134, 140

Saint Petersburg, Russia, 113
Sarah, 64, 76, 78–81, 82, 86, 94
Satan, 96, 139
Saudi Arabia, 97
Scheller, Gustav, 167
second dispersion, 132
Segal, Barry and Batya, 21, 167
Sephardic Jews, 137, 163
shalom, 21, 117–19
Shechem, 142, 146
Sinai, 98, 126
Six-Day War, 126, 142
soberness, 47
Solomon, 32–34, 37–38
South America, 133
Soviet Union, 126, 134, 141
Spain, 163
Star of David, 15
Stearns, Robert, 121, 166
supplication, 134–35, 163
Syria, 96, 97, 98, 126

Temple, 116, 126, 129–30
Ten Commandments, 31
Teplinsky, Sandra, 75, 97
terrorism, 112–13, 143
Titus (Roman ruler), 132
Toward Jerusalem Council II, 167
travail, 50, 163
Treblinka, 109
Truman, Harry S., 111, 112, 141
trumpet, 133
Turkey, 95
Tyre, 98

United Nations, 118, 125, 140
United Prayer Coalition, 166
United States, 111, 140

Vision for Israel, 166
visitation, 163

Waldman, Marty, 167
Watchman International, The, 166
watchmen, 14, 27, 164
watch of the Lord, 163
weeping, 50, 109, 134–35
West Bank, 126, 143
Western (Wailing) Wall, 126
wisdom, 32–34
Word of God, 140–41, 146
World War I, 124
World War II, 124

Yeshua, 23, 86, 101, 118, 164. *See also* Messiah
Yom Kippur, 121
Yom Kippur assault, 126

Zechariah, 15, 16, 116, 146–48
Zion, 18, 114
Zionism, 164